Presentation

What the best presenters know, do and say

second edition

Richard Hall

PEARSON

Prentice Hall

Harlow, England • London • New York • Boston • San Francisco • Toronto • Sydney • Singapore • Hong Kong
Tokyo • Seoul • Taipei • New Delhi • Cape Town • Madrid • Mexico City • Amsterdam • Munich • Paris • Milan

PEARSON EDUCATION LIMITED

Edinburgh Gate
Harlow CM20 2JE
Tel: +44 (0)1279 623623
Fax: +44 (0)1279 431059
Website: www.pearsoned.co.uk

First published 2007
Second edition published in Great Britain in 2008

© Pearson Education Limited 2008

The right of Richard Hall to be identified as author of this work has been asserted
by him in accordance with the Copyright, Designs and Patents Act 1988.

ISBN: 978–0–273–72076–8

British Library Cataloguing-in-Publication Data
A catalogue record for this book is available from the British Library

Library of Congress Cataloging-in-Publication Data
Hall, Richard.
  Brilliant presentation : what the best presenters know, do, and say / Richard
Hall. -- 2nd ed.
    p. cm.
  ISBN 978-0-273-72076-8 (pbk.)
1. Business presentations. 2. Public speaking. I. Title.
  HF5718.22.H35 2008
  658.4'52--dc22

                                                                2008035160

10 9 8 7 6 5 4 3 2 1
12 11 10 09 08

Designed by Sue Lamble
Typeset in 10/14pt Plantin by 3
Printed and bound in Great Britain by Clays Ltd., Bungay, Suffolk

The publisher's policy is to use paper manufactured from sustainable forests.

Endorsements

I strongly believe that being a good communicator is one of the most critical skills required in business today. Presentations are a fundamental part of communications and this is an excellent guide to how to become a brilliant presenter.

Dianne Thompson CBE, Chief Executive of Camelot Group plc

Courage, heart and imagination – a Wizard of Oz journey for everyone who wants to become a brilliant presenter and thinks they'll never get there.

Jeanne-Marie Gescher OBE, Founder and Chief Executive of Claydon Gescher Associates Beijing, China

Brilliant Presentation can make ordinary presentations great and great presentations spectacular. This is a great read – I hope I don't have to compete with anyone who reads it.

Lord Tim Bell, Chairman of Chime Communications

This is a fresh, direct and vivid picture of what it takes to become a very good presenter. Whether you see presenting as a vulnerability of yours or a strength, this book will be genuinely helpful.

Lucy Parker, CEO of Cantos Communications Ltd

We all *think* we know this stuff, but Richard shows us how amateur we really are, and how attention to detail – story, script, illustrative material, slides – can help make an ordinary pitch memorable. Essential reading for anyone who has to make presentations.

James Arnold-Baker, Doctors.net.uk, previously CEO Oxford University Press

At Showcase we have been creating high quality presentations for many years. Successful presenters are rigorous in how they go about developing their presentations, and delivering them. This excellent and accessible book takes you step by step through the process. Strongly recommended.

Martin Conradi, CEO of Showcase Presentations Ltd

Things I've learned are that rather than script a presentation I use evocative words as a signpost for my presentations so each time I rehearse, it is slightly different. This keeps me on my toes so I do my presentation in a story telling manner.

Richard's book provides the key disciplines I use; prepare, relax, engage the audience and enjoy it.

Gary Donaldson, Bid Director for a major Healthcare PFI Project

Contents

Author's acknowledgements

My mission in life – or one of them at any rate – is to help create a generation of truly great and inspirational presenters. I hope this book helps especially as it's been updated and added to in this second edition. It's a well worn truth that you can never stop learning and improving as a presenter or as a writer.

Good presentation, like well presented food, makes life more pleasant for everyone and it sharpens the intellectual taste buds. It isn't, as some have said, vanity. Brilliant presentation, like brilliant advertising, makes things happen; changes minds; increases share price; sells product; saves companies.

My thanks and love to Kate my wife who is my most helpful critic.

Samantha Jackson runs her a close second. It's an interesting job, commissioning editor, involving stick and carrot and a keen sense of seeing the wood for the trees.

She and a large team of excellent people at Pearson do the company and themselves credit by their energy and enthusiasm.

Elie, Lucy, Julie, Kirsty, Laura, Caroline – I salute and thank you for your brilliant support.

Publisher's acknowledgements

We are grateful to the following for permission to reproduce copyright material:

Financial Times, 'Pleasures outweigh the perils of a more balanced commute', 3 July 2006.

Introduction

The importance of presentations

This is about what it takes to be a *brilliant presenter*, how much work you will have to do and why it matters. Being a good presenter has never been more important. Being a brilliant presenter can transform your career.

'In an information economy the ability to convey facts and argument clearly may be the most valuable skill of all'.
Thomas Weber, Stanford University

'Incompetent presentation is tantamount to fraud.'
The Financial Times

It isn't easy – but you can do it

Being a brilliant presenter is not easy. Being a brilliant anything isn't easy. You need some talent, a huge desire to get better, a practical tool kit, a great deal of practice and a lot of hard work and discipline. Becoming a brilliant presenter is not easy.

But this book gives you the basic tool kit, some critical pointers and a lot of words of encouragement. Read it and apply it and I guarantee you will be a good if not brilliant presenter in a few months provided you are prepared to be honest about where you stand in the league table of presenters now and provided you are prepared to put in the hours of practice and homework you will need to help move you up that league table. It should also make you feel relaxed about your quest for excellence and make you realise you start in very good company.

It has always astounded me that so many companies and so many executives assume that presentation is a natural art like walking or running or swimming. Swimming? Take anyone and throw them in the deep end and watch them swim ... or, more likely, drown. Like swimming, presenting is something you learn. Some are innately good at it and think nothing of standing up in front of a room of people and talking to them. If you are one of those lucky few you still need to read this book because then you might, just might, become a brilliant presenter, a gold medal orator. Most, however, will flail desperately, swallow water, go blue in the face, panic and drown.

A cruel form of torture – the 'P' word

All you have to do is walk into a room and shout *'presentation time'* to reduce half the people there to quivering wrecks. One person I coached found it hard to remember their own name and what their job was when made to stand up in a room empty of other people apart from me. I could even see their legs quaking. To them, sudden and unexpected death would have been preferable to this torture.

So we have the two issues that impede a brilliant or even, simply, a competent presentation being delivered:

● Nerves so bad they create what I call 'panic drowners';
● Lack of knowledge as to what to do. This breed is very common – and I call these 'non-swimmers'.

Rob Harper, a swimming coach, tells me there is a third category – what he calls the 'silent drowner' who simply and miserably takes in a lot of water and sinks without trace.

There are quite a few presenters like that too.

What happens if you can't present well

So does presenting matter? A former chief executive of Rentokil said memorably after a particularly heavily criticised presentation to analysts: 'I'm paid to be a CEO not an actor'. Shortly afterwards, because of analyst reaction to his presentation, he was fired.

We are, all of us, exposed daily to very competent presentation by people called newsreaders and hosts on chat shows. We have a benchmark. It is no longer acceptable to appear nervous or shifty or lost for words. We must not be what high court judges sometimes describe as an 'unreliable witness'.

The so-called 'transparency' of contemporary life wherein more managers and company leaders are simply asked more and more questions is one where the ability to stand up and talk fluently about almost anything and, more importantly, stand up for your company with clarity and command, is the least we all expect.

In reality, competent presentation matters a lot. Investors in companies take a lot of notice of the confidence and conviction with which a leader talks about his company and its plans. How else, they argue, can they tell what the real prospects are? If the chief is uncertain about what is going on, or if it seems he or she is probably spinning them a lie, why on earth should they put that precious pension money at risk in his or her care? A senior analyst told me that he wanted 'to see the whites of their eyes'.

In other words, a brilliant presentation.

In saying this he fairly represented the confrontational nature of the analyst–manager relationship. I hope he wasn't tempted to shoot them as the original saying went (was it General Custer?) 'Wait until you see the whites of their eyes – then let them have it.' Nicola Horlick of Balliol and City fame said something similar about wanting to look into the eyes of executives to see if they were lying to her. Jeremy Paxman, in contrast, doesn't need to look into any politician's eyes because he starts from the assumption that 'this bastard's lying to me – it's up to me to find out about what'.

And if presentation has a slightly dodgy reputation it's because people such as Alistair Campbell and Philip Gould, the architects of New Labour, have created a new level of aggressive spin that makes many uncertain of what is true and forces us to presume all politicians are probably guilty of mendacious behaviour.

The 'must haves' in business today

Away from the increasing murky and spinning-a-line world of politics, however, there's a short list of must-haves if you want to get on in life. Here's the checklist for candidates:

● Can they read?
● Can they write?
● Can they add up?
● Can they think?
● Can they perform simple tasks consistently?
● Can they do what they are told?
● Can they present?

Presenting is taught as a normal skill at many schools now. Would that we non-swimmers had been so lucky.

Presentations are normal nowadays

At almost every level of every company the need to do a presentation of some sort will occur quite often. This could be a simple speech of thanks – that's a presentation – or a description of the activities of your department to a visitor – that's a presentation too – or the story about the new marketing campaign accompanied by visual aids and music – and that is a *big* presentation.

Regard this book, at its lowest level of use, as an insurance policy. Buy it, read it and when the call to present comes you'll be fine, provided you follow the advice it contains. But if you aspire to being the person who is constantly asked to present stuff because you are so good at it that people describe you as 'brilliant' then read, mark, learn, inwardly digest and practise like mad. I have sought to make the book simple, easy to read and practical.

Most of all, I recognise that there are different levels of competence. I do not follow the school of advice that makes bold assumptions like the cookery book that said: '*Fillet your dover sole then cover in flour . . .*' Hang on! Fillet? How do you do that?

We are going to go through this step by step and start at the beginning. If that's too basic for you, then you can jump to the appropriate level.

Good luck. Your first step towards being a brilliant presenter has already been taken. You are reading the most up-to-date, practical and simplest 'how to' book on the subject.

CHAPTER 1

The stuff of brilliant presentations

What, in simple terms, is a brilliant presentation? If you have only five minutes to get your act together, then read this. It tells you how to achieve radical improvements. This is what they call the 'executive summary'.

Fires

How do you actually do a 'brilliant presentation' – once you have controlled your nerves? (Study Chapter 2 now for advice on this). I've talked to people who used templates, who recycled old presentations, who scoured *Old Bloaters' Book of Favourite Jokes and One Liners*, and I have to say I always thought it showed. Write these brilliant five words on the wall.

FRESH INFORMATIVE RELEVANT

ENTHUSIASTIC STORY

If you like acronyms, call this the 'Fires' approach. If you don't then just *think* about these five words. Whatever else you do, you just have to be able to put a tick next to each one when you've got your next presentation ready.

brilliant tips

- Fresh. Whatever else you do, make your material sound new, original and fresh. Try to find a couple of interesting insights. Gigantic facts can help, for instance 'All the beans Heinz sells every year would fill Wembley Stadium up to row N' sounds better than some tonnage figure. Most of all, in saying 'fresh' I'm demanding an attitude of mind that leads to every show being seen as a new show and every audience being regarded as a new audience.

- Informative. There are many occasions (such as in a wedding speech) when good-natured entertainment is the limit of most people's ambitions. But in a business environment any presentation that doesn't provide new information, or a new interpretation of existing information, isn't doing its job. Our job in business is to change things and move them on. There'll be a lot to read about the power of clear and powerful delivery and dramatic slides in this book but, when it comes to the crunch, content is what makes the difference, not spin.

- Relevant. Don't give a presentation that is not relevant to the audience or to the circumstances in which they and the company find themselves. Examine what you are going to say with utter ruthlessness. Keep on asking 'is this relevant?' If it isn't, bin it.

- Enthusiastic. The word 'passion' is overused in business because it makes people who should know better behave with inappropriate zeal and with excessively evangelical language. This is not a church outing. This is a business. We are selling cough drops or whatever, we are not selling salvation. But we should enjoy what we do. It makes us a better company. Being enthusiastic is more appealing to an audience. It also improves the pace and vitality of communication.

- Story. We can argue that there are many types of presentation, but really there is only one – the one that tells a story with a beginning, a middle and an end. The context in which that story is told will vary, as will the audience and their expectations, but without a story to tell you shouldn't be presenting at all. I chair a charity organisation and I have banned the use of 'mission statement' and had it replaced by the simpler 'our story'. It's easier to spin a mission statement (in corporate speak) than it is to spin a story because stories are told to seven-year-olds and they won't put up with nonsense and prevarication.

What we now need is a prescriptive set of actions to perform in creating our 'brilliant presentation'.

Five critical processes

These are the five key headings that you have to follow. Do what you will – stop reading the book now, throw it out of the window, burn it, eat it – but whatever else you do, *please* do these five things.

1 Decide very clearly the *context* of your presentation.
2 Get your *key story* down to a cryptic message.
3 Develop facts around your story that give it *colour*.
4 Illustrate your story with brilliant *visuals* – or use none at all.
5 *Perform* your presentation with power and pace.

I once watched a presenter guiding a presentation along a path to a soggy mess and I wondered why his multinational employer hadn't recognised that presenting was vital in his job. Why didn't they teach the poor executive how to swim? Presenting a story or argument to an audience is a learned skill and not an innate gift for nine out of ten people. But it's a really important one.

brilliant tip

Presenting a story to an audience brilliantly is a skill you learn, not an innate gift

brilliant example

Jack Welch, the brilliant former chief of the US company General Electric, got it more right than most when he said: 'I always thought that chart-making clarified my thinking better than anything else. Reducing a complex problem to a simple chart excited the hell out of me.'

CHAPTER 2

Coping with nerves

Controlling your nerves (if you have them, and nearly everyone does) is the biggest step you can make towards being good at and enjoying presenting. To control them you must understand them and realise that nerves are normal. You must also realise that controlling them is a must for anyone who aspires to brilliance.

Nerves are normal

I am putting this subject right up front because to many people the whole business of doing a presentation, or indeed any solo performance in front of an audience, causes physical anguish so great that it is disabling.

The former chief of a major multinational told me that he'd cried himself to sleep following an inaugural speech he'd made at his new company – ruined by his faltering and then stuttering and drying up. He said that he'd felt like a high performance Italian car running out of fuel on a motorway.

There is little point in talking about the finer points of presenting if the prospective presenter or victim (because this is how they feel) wants to get it over and done with before bursting into tears or worse.

It's the voice that is key

In Julie Stanford's excellent compendium *The Essential Business Guide*, Chris Davidson gives some great advice. He notes that 'the voice is an excellent barometer of the body's overall level of nervousness'. He recommends the following:

- Hold good posture.
- Breathe from the diaphragm.
- Keep the voice well lubricated with water.
- Do a warm-up – especially making '...ng' sounds as in 'bring' or 'bang'.
- Pronounce whole words.
- Relax the face and shoulders (especially the neck and shoulders).

This is great stuff and I endorse it – especially the advice on posture and relaxation.

How to avoid freezing

The voice coach Valentine Palmer also focuses on confidence. He talks about 'freezing', 'losing your way', 'your voice letting you down at a crucial moment'.

A presenter freezing is like an actor drying or a golfer with the yips. It is not something that anyone who has conquered it wants to talk about because, like blushing, it is hopefully a thing of the past.

You avoid freezing by keeping light on your feet, moving around and telling yourself: 'This will be OK.' Cars don't freeze up until the oil runs out. Keeping talking to yourself is the equivalent of lubrication. You avoid losing your way by ensuring that you keep signposts and a roadmap in front of you – your script or notes will do that.

Your voice is your best friend or your worst enemy. Make sure that you water it on the stage – frequently. If it seems about to give up in a croak say something like: 'After too much talking recently my voice is beginning to give in . . . I, however, am not.'

brilliant tip

Your voice is your best friend or your worst enemy

I want to dwell on this issue of nerves at some length because as long as you feel a 'confidence crisis' you will find presenting hard. You may survive an encounter with a presentation if you are very, very nervous but it is unlikely that you'll ever get beyond being graded as 'quite good' until you are in command of yourself and, especially, until you are in command of your voice.

There are exceptions of course. Arthur Rubinstein used to be sick before going on stage to play the piano . . . he had to be pushed reluctantly on. Then he played the piano and he was wonderful! Many great actors are quivering wrecks before a performance.

So how do brilliant presenters feel?

There may be a tingle or two and a rush of adrenalin but none of that wild-eyed, dry-mouthed croaking and freezing that has blighted so many careers. However, I know of no accomplished presenter who cannot take a deep breath and, using any or all of the techniques I'll describe, not be in a state of self-control before a performance and *enjoy* going for it.

I heard of one female executive who lost it so badly that she froze and stared manically at the bemused audience before screaming 'Stop it! Stop it! Just stop looking at me like that . . .' before rushing off. Poor thing – she had acute 'presentationitis' which, while not life-threatening, is definitely career-threatening and very, very nasty. So how do we cure this?

Be honest with yourself

You have to start by being totally honest with yourself and others.

- How bad is your problem? Write it down now in detail.
- Describe how really awful you feel when it's at its worst.
- What is the worst it's ever been? No, confess to really the absolute worst.
- Analyse how you felt – top to toe and top to bottom.
  - how was your mouth?
  - how was your voice?
  - how were your knees?
  - how was your face?
  - could you see clearly?
  - how was your stomach?
  - how was your head?
- How did you feel about the situation you were in?

Just facing up to all this will make a huge difference and stop you hiding from the problem.

What is actually going on?

These acute attacks of nerves have been described and analysed in great detail by squads of experts. Treatment is very much the norm, although left untreated such attacks can lead eventually to agoraphobia, which is much more serious.

The symptoms include shaking, a racing heart, sweating, difficulty catching breath, chest pain, dizziness, tingling in the hands and nausea, or more extremely (according to *The Analyst*) a palpable, screaming fear rising inside you.

Attacks are more frequent in winter than summer and more common in women than men. Common indications include changes in blood pH levels, which is suggestive of hyperventilation. Apparently, breathing more slowly or breathing into a paper bag can restore normal pH levels.

What actually happens? The brain has a small structure called the amygdala which can act as an 'anxiety switch' that flips on only when anxiety seems necessary – when you face a tiger, a raging torrent or the prospect of a presentation. No I'm not joking – presentations are one of the commonest reasons for the switch being turned on. When it is turned on adrenaline and serotonin are released making the body – going back to our primate beginnings – ready for escape. Adrenaline is also known as the 'fight or flight' hormone. It speeds everything up – the heart beats faster and blood is redirected to the muscles making you better able to fight or run away. In addition, the brain shuts down – in a life-or-death crisis you need instinct not brains. The problem is that the opposite is desirable during a presentation – you need your brain to work for you.

Serotonin is much more complex and in the most extreme situations can kill you. Think of the effect of magic mushrooms and you'll get the idea. It passes around your system very efficiently and quickly creating euphoria, over-reaction of the reflexes and a happy drunken state. If you are lucky this makes you feel ready to take on the world, but if you are unlucky it can make you feel as though you are about to die of a heart attack.

So now we sort of know what is going on, let's do something about it.

Be self-aware

I am neither a doctor nor psychiatrist but having done hundreds of presentations I know that the most powerful tool that you have in preparing for a presentation is self-awareness. If you were flying a plane you'd go through a routine in which you check if everything is working properly. And it is a routine – an unfailing do-it-in-this-order-every-time routine. This is what *you* must do before you present.

There are a few exercises that may help you, but the chances are you will benefit from working with a professional presentation

brilliant tip

The most powerful tool that you have in preparing for a presentation is self-awareness

coach – especially if you are really suffering from anticipatory nerves to the point of feeling unwell.

Do you find that prospect humiliating? Well I guess you did have driving lessons? Yes? Well presenting is much more dangerous than driving.

To be nervous is normal

The body has the most brilliant defence and drug drip-feed system imaginable. You just need to understand what is going on to help to manage the effects and control them.

Everyone gets nervous. Actually that's not entirely true. Some people *claim* to be free of nerves and, surprise surprise, they are nearly always hopeless presenters – overbearing, too loud and self-obsessed.

Feeling nervous is good – used properly, nerves are our 'presentation muscles'. Flexing them gives us a 'hyper-performance' feel that takes us from an ordinary to an extraordinary level of audience control.

The line to be drawn is between:

- 'acutely self-aware and ready to rock' – this is brilliant;
- 'shivering with apprehension and wanting to go to the loo' – this is bad, very bad.

So how do you get to the first state of grace and avoid the second?

Everyone has nerves. The best, or at any rate the most prag-

brilliant tips

To help control your nerves

- Practise breathing in and out. Big breath in, count to four; then breathe out, count to eight. Repeat this four times. Critically, the breaths out are twice as long as those in.

- Sing your nerves away. Anyone who has been unfortunate enough to have had a stutter knows only too well that this affliction happens when talking and never when singing. Try going into the bathroom and belting out a big song, or your presentation message to some kind of rap beat.

- Externalise. This was the trick that got me off the 'if-there-was-only-a-hole-to swallow-me-up' feeling. I did a little con trick on myself and said 'imagine I could fly out of myself'. So I did a little psychological flight up into the roof beams and looked down at myself. Watching me down there put everything into perspective. I felt quite cheerful – and I performed well.

- Feel comfortable. If you feel good you will generally do well. You simply feel in charge of yourself and those around you. Ronald Reagan might have been just a 'B' actor but he was an

undoubted 'A*' when it came to confidence. It was said of
Ronald that 'he felt comfortable in his shoes'. Next time you
present, make sure you wear your comfiest shoes – and I do
mean your comfiest and not your smartest.

- Practise in the nude. David Heslop is a former chief of both
  Mazda and Expotel and this is his idea. The idea is that you get
  a full length mirror, strip naked and practise your presentation
  in front of it. Now David is really quite a large man but that
  merely adds weight to his argument that if you can do
  something as embarrassing as this with a straight face then a
  full auditorium will be nothing in comparison.

- Think about your audience. The certain knowledge of what the
  audience might think about you may shape your content, your
  delivery and certainly your confidence. Try this exercise. Imagine
  that you have to go into two separate rooms – a blue room and
  a red room. You have a presentation to deliver entitled 'How I
  learned to become a confident presenter'.

  - In the blue room is an audience of the most intimidating
    teachers from school and also your current and all (yes *all*)
    your previous bosses, and anyone else in your life who has
    intimidated you.

  - In the red room is an audience of relatively well-behaved
    eleven-year-olds whom you don't know, but you do know
    that they have been told that you are a nice person. Now I
    want you to work out exactly how and why your
    performance will be different in front of the two audiences
    and why the eleven-year-olds may see you differently from
    the historic ogres. The difference in *your* feeling from each
    audience may help unlock your inbuilt 'confidence machine'.

- Preparation creates the confidence of the professional
  presenter. When you watch a brilliant presenter at work and

wonder how they do it, you need to remember that they have probably worked much harder at putting it all together than you could imagine. As a rule of thumb assume you are a senior manager planning an important presentation:

- the initial writing should take about three hours;

- the refinements about the same – three hours;

- your stage one slide construction – two hours;

- examining the slides you have had done professionally (it's worth it) – two hours;

- the rehearsals and rewrites – another three hours;

- going back to the drawing board and consulting with colleagues – three hours;

- coaching on performance – three hours.

Does nineteen hours seem too long? It isn't – ask a professional. What all this preparation does is enhance your confidence and your chances of success hugely.

- Don't drink before you present. I'm told a 'shot of vodka' is the answer. It isn't. Don't do it – ever. Any more than you'd expect your surgeon to drink ('just to steady my hands') before an operation. While it may seem the answer for this particular presentation, in your stoned state you won't learn why what went well went well, and why what didn't didn't. Remember 'Lucky Jim' where Jim got horrendously drunk before a presentation? Never, ever do it.

- Lying down and other exercises. If you get those dreadful 'Why am I doing this?' 'May the world swallow me up' feelings do the following:

  - slow down;

- breathe deeply, 4–8–4–8;

- lie down ... this can really help;

- practise lip manoeuvres to loosen your mouth muscles;

- visualise yourself on-form and doing well;

- lie down again – close your eyes and breathe like you've never breathed before;

- do voice exercises to get your vocal cords working;

- make sure your mouth and lips are moist.

- You are not going to die. Lucy Kellaway wrote about cycling to work in the *Financial Times* on 3 July 2006, 'Despite the risk I hardly ever feel frightened on my bike. I feel alert and alive but not scared. Recently I was cycling out one hot evening to give a speech to some business people. I was feeling fine about the ride but not about the impending talk. On the way I was nearly hit by a passenger door being flung open, I swerved and narrowly avoided a van. I put the thought to myself "how come I'm not frightened of being crushed to death but I'm terrified of minor humiliation in front of a small audience of civilised people". Suddenly I wasn't frightened any more. On the stage sweaty palms are no longer a problem.'

matic, among us controls them and uses them. Be pragmatic whatever else – the luckiest enjoy their nerves. Like Frank Skinner enjoys a really hot curry. A bit uncomfortable, but boy, doesn't it make you aware of your own body and your own mortality.

Summary

Once conquered, those very nerves that disabled your earlier performances as a presenter can turn you from novice to master. Controlling those nerves and using the tips above will help you learn how to do astonishing and exciting stuff. Recognise that skating brilliantly involves the prospect of falling (and remember that falling isn't failing).

Presenting is high octane dangerous – so you are right to be nervous anyway. At its best it's scary but nice. But whichever way always a bit scary. But do it well and the post-presentational euphoria is a great sensation. How dangerous is it? Here's what Stephen Spielberg said about it: 'We had snakes in *The Raiders of the Lost Ark*, bugs in *Indiana Jones and the Temple of Doom*. But supposedly man's greatest fear is public speaking. That'll be in our next picture.'

We're still waiting Stephen. It'll make *Psycho* look like *Mary Poppins*.

CHAPTER 3

The five levels
of mastery

This chapter describes the five levels you can achieve as a presenter – as you will see, most people don't get beyond level one. The whole point here is that it's hard to be competent let alone good and very hard to be brilliant. The key is to be honest about where you think you are starting on this journey of improvement.

This is not an easy journey. You can't suddenly leap up and proclaim 'I want to be a film star' and be one. It will require work, practice, effort and a lot of blood, sweat and tears. Forget the blood – sweat and tears will do.

First of all let's describe the stages on the journey.

The world of the non-presenter

Before we talk about the levels of mastery themselves, we have to agree there are those who never have and feel that they never could deliver a presentation. These probably represent more than half of the population. This is nothing to be ashamed of, nor is it something to worry about.

Even if you are one of these, something will happen to you once you've taken the book's advice on how to draft and deliver a simple presentation. About half of you will still hate it and find it nerve-racking, but don't worry because you *will* grow to enjoy it. The other half will get bitten by the presentation bug. You'll experience the serious sense of power as you control a room of people and focus on working an audience. You will scarcely be able to wait before your next presentation or speech. You have entered that most dangerous of phases called 'new' – as in new driver, new golfer, new jogger. You are likely to sweep all before you, terrify passers-by and be alternately full and devoid of confidence. Your body will become full of adrenaline, serotonin and nerves.

But if you want to progress, here are the steps you need to take and a description of what reaching each level requires.

Five steps to brilliance

I've created these five levels because to improve you have to know where you start. Imagine life without examinations, a career without promotion and a progression up the hierarchy, imagine a world where everything was the same – forever.

So be aware of where you start. In all the presentation coaching programmes I run, whether it's modesty or acute self criticism, few people rate themselves as a presenter. We are about to change that.

Step one: novice presenter

Surprisingly few people make it beyond this point. I call them 'weekend presenters' – people who do the odd presentation and can cope perfectly competently with small groups. They are good at their job, be it junior brand manager, personnel executive or management accountant. Presentations are neither very important to them nor are they especially nervous at the prospect of addressing a breakout group.

They tend to 'busk it' and a few hours before their presentation do their own PowerPoint slides crammed with bullet points – 'a script on the screen' there to help the presenter not the audience.

They make a virtue out of the low key provision of information. At all costs they avoid the risk of what I call 'theatrical performance' because this increases the potential for greater failure.

If they are asked if they want lights, make-up, autocue and a sound system, or if they are told that they'll be talking to an audience of one hundred, or that this can be career-shaping then the nerves will probably start to kick in.

It's important to recognise that these people are probably pretty good communicators with their peers. But they'd much rather communicate with them in small and relatively informal groups – sitting down rather than standing up.

It's also important that we don't criticise them for achieving only level one. It's a rule of this book, and life, that you need to try to get better but that it is far better being a brilliant presenter at this level than a neurotic at level two.

However, there are things they can think about if they are going to improve:

brilliant tips

- As a novice, focus on de-cluttering slides so they are clearer and simpler for the audience to interact with.
- Discard slides if the presentation is to a small group.
- Give the presentation a splash of colour.
- Think about what exactly it is they want to achieve – outcomes not just inputs.
- Think about the audience.

What level-one presenters should do now (you may be beginning to feel that you fall into this category by now) is review their last three presentations to see if they made sense, whether they could have been better, how they'd do them differently/better, and how they would cope if they were now asked to do a big presentation to senior management at a conference.

They may survive perfectly well as a novice but stepping up to the next level won't harm their career prospects.

Step two: apprentice presenter

Getting to the level of apprentice presenter is, in golfing terms, the equivalent of playing off 18 and regularly breaking 90. In cooking terms it's equivalent to being able to do anything that Jamie Oliver throws at you – dinner parties hold no terrors.

Apprentice presenters are competent. They know how to put together half-decent slides and a well-argued story. They suffer from nerves but remain in control. They've probably done about ten presentations, of which about half have been at all-singing, all-dancing sales events and audiences have been generous in their praise.

They realise they should have spent more time on preparation, but they are very busy people and the thing that gets left till last is always the presentation. They know that their slides are a bit dull and last time out they decided to build in a more visual approach, but when the slide showing a herd of gazelle bolting across a plain came up they couldn't remember what it was supposed to signify – so they said 'these deer are frightened just like our competitors'. This got a laugh but made little sense when the next slide that came up said 'the competitive threat – why we should worry'.

Level-two presenters are ambitious and realise that their prospects can be enhanced by being a bit more adept. There are several things they need to think about.

brilliant tips

- An apprentice should spend a lot more time on preparation.

- Go for a visual approach but with a verbal clue – having 'victim or predator?' on the gazelle slide might have helped the flow – and, by the way, they *are* gazelle *not* deer, that was just careless.

- Script themselves more tightly, especially as they move to more staged events.

- Work on the beginning, the end and the killer central slide if they are to graduate to the next level.

- Probably lighten up a little.

Step three: craftsman presenter

At this level, presentation skills will affect their career progress. They will be asked to give speeches at events, and others will be glad to know that such a craftsman is speaking at a conference.

It is widely recognised that they are confident and competent, and that they are completely reliable. They are courteous to technicians and they deliver stylish, well-thought out presentations which reflect how much time, effort and creativity has been spent. In fact, they now spend a huge amount of time preparing – probably an increasing amount for each presentation they do. They keep a 'presentation box' at home into which interesting cuttings, pictures or cartoons go. They have a book of great quotations. They have become a management book junkie. Doing presentations has now become a hobby.

Craftsmen presenters promote themselves as industry experts with a view to being candidates for invitations to international events – *What's New 2002?* in Las Vegas, a think-in for senior managers; *The Innovation Forum* in St Lucia 2004; *New Wave*

Thinking in the New World in Shanghai 2006; *Why Dubai?* 2007;
After Tom Peters . . . Reframing the Work of a Player in Buenos Aires
2008; *New Frontiers, New Thinking Ladders* in Sydney 2009.
Their speeches have been assembled in a short book by Prentice
Hall entitled *The Craft of Originality* so these craftsmen's reputa-
tions are made.

But they are still only level-three craftsmen. If they were to see this
rating they'd probably say, somewhat indignantly, 'but everyone
says I am brilliant'. Maybe, but sometimes a bit dull, perhaps a bit
second-hand. A bit – no, not just a bit – *much* too safe, too solidly
in their comfort zone. They're very good but they aren't great.

They no longer get a flutter of nerves when they present. They
are in perfect control. They are urbane, funny, supremely confident and consistent. They too have several things they could
address to reach the next level.

brilliant tips

- A craftsman should carry on presenting – they like doing it and
  the audience seems to like them.

- Ask themselves a searching question – what are they achieving?

- Reflect on whether or not their company – which is subsidising
  their activities – deserves a bigger shout in the messages being
  put out. Are they selling the company hard enough? Or are they
  selling *themselves*?

- Try to be more exciting, frightening, dramatic – anything to get
  themselves out of the safety box they are in.

- Work with others to raise their game – if they were golfers we'd
  be wanting to get them down to low single figures.

- Try to do one controversial and challenging presentation that
  puts them under a bit of pressure.

Step four: star presenter

This is the most dangerous level of all. At their very best they are Oscar winners and incomparably talented – at their worst they are just dreadful. They suffer agonies as though their stomachs were being eaten alive by ferrets before any performance. They are horrible to everyone around them before they perform – technicians, friends, colleagues, lovers, wives – everyone. They want to change everything at the last minute – always.

Star presenters give 'prima donna' new meaning. They are supremely confident or utterly devoid of confidence. They are a mess of extremes – happy, sad, energetic, inert, loving, vindictive, inclusive, divisive. They are very focused on what they want. They have a very short attention span. They have blasts of huge creativity and then get stuck for days. They cry in private and sometimes in public too. They consistently feel sorry for themselves. Their emotional age is seven. They are often chief executives.

What they are blessed with is the rare and magic gift of being able to communicate a vision or personal dream in a language that resonates with the audience. They use beautifully simple language and short sentences – really short.

Level-four presenters work with the best slide artists – those who can make a dull graph jive, who can animate the description of an operational process to make people's mouths fall open in comprehension, who make audiences want to look at that screen just to enjoy the spectacle of vivid logic unfolding before them.

Level-four presenters are presentational professionals and human relations amateurs – brilliant but impossible. The reason they don't quite make level five is their selfishness and erratic behaviour. If you see yourself in this characterisation I have two things to say – congratulations, you clearly have huge talent.

Now do the following if you want to become truly and consistently brilliant.

brilliant tips

- Not much you can say to a star except calm down.

- Learn the tone of voice and look that you want to project and take it from there – the late Sir Laurence Olivier used to say once he had got the walk and the clothes right everything else followed.

- Learn consistency – it will give you a longer life and earn you more friends.

- Use the most important words in management, 'thank you' and 'well done', more often. The team around you can help to lift your game on your off days and to make you fly on your good days. They need to be appreciated.

- Think more about your audience than you currently do.

- Stop showing off so much.

- Control your nerves – you might only be brilliant now by the skin of your teeth and that sounds like fragile success.

Step five: brilliant presenter

Congratulations! Join a cadre of the elite – Bill Clinton, Tim Bell, Tony O'Reilly, Alan Parker, Tom Peters, Richard Eyres, Tony Blair, Charles Handy, Michael Portillo – and, currently, a few others.

The idea, of course, is that books like this which are dedicated to the improvement of presentation skills, will make 'brilliance' a less unattainable peak. In 1953 Everest was scaled for the first time – in May 2006 nearly 200 people climbed it.

Like flu, brilliance is catching.

This is what brilliance is

I define brilliance in presentation as comprising:

- A deep, transcendental knowledge.
- An all-consuming passion for the subject.
- The ability to tell a story in simple language.
- The ability to make a story seem fresh and full of a sense of discovery.
- A sense of pace and control – a busy person bestowing their time on you.

It's asking a lot of the brilliant presenter that they always be brilliant but once they've set the standard we should expect no less of them. And sometimes a star, or even craftsman, presenter can attain brilliance. Take Melvyn Bragg (a good craftsman presenter I'd thought) – I saw him once on stage in Brighton talking about his book *Twelve Books that Changed the World*. He was a revelation, fizzing with enthusiasm and boyish excitement. He was hopelessly lacking in discipline and ran over time, but he spoke from the depths of knowledge and discovery that drive him as a person. It was like hearing Eric Clapton playing a long improvised riff – totally brilliant.

Brilliant presenters are shameless

Brilliant presenters should polish their craft and coach those around them. There is too little constructive talk about how to create great presentations, yet this is what often elevates debate about a subject and the advancement of human understanding.

Being a brilliant presenter may be an attainment closer for you than you had ever thought possible. Nine out of ten presenters don't get better because they don't try and can't be bothered. Think about it – could you be one of these wretches?

Summary

It's possible you won't reach the peak of brilliance as a presenter but it has to be worth trying. And as that legendary advertising man Leo Burnett said: 'If you reach for the stars at least you won't end up with a handful of dust.'

The most important advice is to be ambitious. To want to get really good at it. In short, to go for it.

I asked Will Arnold Baker, head of client services at advertising agency Publicis what he thought constituted brilliance in presenting. He said that some of the best that he'd seen were utterly shameless (that word again), that to them this was 'show-time' and that they'd say anything and make up anything to achieve a good effect. To them, applause was all that mattered.

CHAPTER 4

The context of the presentation

f you don't know *why* you are doing a presentation, *where* you are doing it, *when* you are doing it, to *whom* you are doing it, *what* the state of the political or commercial climate is, *what* the audience knows already and *what* they expect then expect to fail – unless, of course, you are very, very lucky.

Have you got the plot?

Understanding the context in which your presentation will take place is the biggest factor in determining whether or not you can become a brilliant presenter. It's a simple rule of life that if you don't know what's going on you are unlikely to be successful. Understand the exact reason for a presentation, the occasion of its happening, the desires and needs of the audience, the local and world situation, the company's latest news, gossip within the company – never underestimate this – and you may find that a mediocre piece of work can go down a storm.

brilliant tip

It's a simple rule of life that if you don't know and understand what's going on around you that you are unlikely to be successful

The effect of context is mighty. What may be a fantastic presentation on day one may sink like a stone on another – the all-important audience reaction is always about context. So how do you avoid getting it wrong and how, on a more positive note, do you make sure you get it right?

First, get the exam question right

It seems pretty obvious, but do your presentation on the subject you've been asked to talk about. Auberon Waugh was apparently ready, at a price, to talk about anything, anytime and anywhere in the world. However, he misheard the organiser of a particular conference over the phone – all he heard really was the word 'Tuscany' followed shortly by the words 'pounds' and 'thousands'. He was then startled to be asked to talk about breast feeding. Nonetheless, Tuscany is Tuscany and thousands of pounds are thousands of pounds so he conscientiously researched the subject about which he knew nothing. It was only in Florence as he was about to deliver that he discovered he was supposed to be talking about press freedom. An easy mistake to make – especially if you are slightly deaf and rather avaricious.

It's astonishing how often this 'exam question problem' is got wrong. Here is a set of planning questions you should ask, and have answered, if you are to maximise your chances of doing yourself justice and being brilliant.

brilliant tips

The checklist

1   What is the event about?

   ● Why is it happening?

   ● Who decided to set it up?

   ● What is the agenda?

   ● Is there a hidden agenda?

- What is the organiser hoping to achieve?

- What is the parent company doing currently?

- What issues is the company facing – commercially, competitively, strategically, financially, politically, in staff turnover terms, in terms of management stability, new brooms or old brooms, bad news, good news, scandals?

2 What about the people in the audience?

- Do they like each other?

- What happened last time this group got together? Did they stick around afterwards?

- Was the event a success or a failure?

- Are there any underlying tensions? While running one offsite presentation I found the atmosphere very strange. It transpired that the chief and his deputy were at loggerheads, so much so that one would probably have to leave the business. Their colleagues were taking sides. No one had thought to mention this in briefing me.

- What do the people in the audience do? Are they your subordinates, peers or superiors?

- Does anyone know what they think, what their problems are and what they expect from you and this meeting?

- Do they know you or of you? If so, what does this knowledge comprise? If not, what is their expectation likely to be?

- Can you get to meet any of them before you speak? David Heslop (ex-chief Mazda and Expotel) was asked to speak to the sales people from the *Independent*. He prepared his presentation and then realised that it was full of him, what he thought, his industry not theirs and that if he did get through to them at all then that it would be purely coincidental. He happens to be a good pianist so he arrived a day early and played piano in the hotel bar where, incognito, he got to know many of the *Independent* people. When he spoke next day he did so knowledgeably and as an insider. He was a 'wow'.

3   What size of audience?

●   How many will there be in the audience? This is critical – there are broadly four kinds of audience size:

a.   intimate meeting (under 10): a sit down, relatively informal environment with, hopefully, plenty of interaction. A flip chart or overhead projector can work well, but avoid elaborate and expensive visual aids.

b.   big meeting (10–30): this is a reasonably formal meeting with fairly strict rules of engagement, which nonetheless will need plenty of back and forth conversation if it is to achieve high energy. This can be a brilliant forum for achieving big realignment of company thinking or strategy.

c.   on stage (30–100): now we are beginning to talk 'theatre'. You need a stage, good lighting, sound systems and decent visuals. You'll need to have a carefully crafted speech. You may be less likely to improvise and you will need to be more careful.

d.   theatre (100+): at this level we are talking about all the tricks of the trade. You need professional back-up, and if you don't have it in spades then you aren't being professional. Spend at least as much time on rehearsing in situ as you would rehearsing in total for a smaller event. This is high risk and high reward. Someone from Unilever told me about 'the good old days' at the Palladium when top management was expected to perform alongside the likes of Tommy Cooper and Eric Morecambe at big sales presentations. Now that really is challenging stuff.

- A big 'show' is also a big test of you as a manager. If you don't know exactly how that theatre or that stage is going to *feel* then you are running as big a risk as someone going on a journey to a place they've never been before without a map.

4 Where are things heading?

- Think really hard about the present and the future. We are living in a world of profound change. As Leonard Riggio of Barnes and Noble put it in *Fast Company*, 'Everything is in play.' This means that no presentation made to a management group can have much credibility unless it reflects the scale and pace of current change. You should start every presentation with: 'Are you sitting comfortably? Well you shouldn't be.'

- There are many good examples. Google is talking about its developments being constrained by the speed of light! The size of China is put into context when I tell you its disabled population is the same as the total UK population! McDonalds finds it quicker, cheaper and more efficient to outsource its customer ordering than to do it on the premises! Hedge funds are now so big that collectively they will, in effect, run the world economy shortly! (Or not. The credit crunch of 2007/8 might have put paid to them. All of which goes to show that there is no certainty in anything nowadays except in the primacy of genuine talent.) The older consumers will kill marketing as we know it because by now they all know how it works – 'pull the other one Paul Daniels!' Most of the technology we rely on today will be redundant by 2010! Big corporations are doomed – they just take a long time to die! Don't know how to use the web? Expire dinosaur!

● So are you fully up to speed with the context of the markets in which you operate? You need to be because no one wants to listen to anyone who is out of date.

5   Are you up to speed on the day itself?

By this I mean with what is going on in the news – not just in your business. I was once doing an offsite presentation to a strategy group. As I drove to the meeting I heard the dire news of 'Black Wednesday' unfolding with Norman *'je ne regrette rien'* Lamont, addressing the media as interest rates soared. The poor souls at my presentation, having been locked away, knew nothing of this until I told them. From that point on nothing else mattered to them. They all sat quietly and miserably considering their newly unaffordable mortgages. Context is everything.

6   Where is it and what is the agenda?

● In the office, close by, luxury hotel, overnight, abroad, big or small location?

● What sort of room?

● What sort of equipment?

● Do you have any say in what can be changed?

● Do you trust the people running it?

● Will it be hot or cold? Whatever it is make sure you are comfortable and confident – a tight suit and tie in 35°C is a bad idea. I once gave a presentation to a global advertising conference in the Martinez in Cannes. Very hot. Sweltering at 2pm in my room I abandoned my carefully prepared presentation. I focused on how I looked and the impression I gave. I went 'mafia'. Dark glasses. Black suit. Open-necked, white linen shirt. Rumpled, bedroom hair. They loved the creative look. I talked creatively ... few words, lots of asides, lots of audience contact. I spoke what we now call 'bloke'. We connected. It worked.

- Who comes before and after you? How is the audience likely to be feeling as you come on – bored, asleep, dead, excited, argumentative, angry, fed up, happy, expectant, relieved? Whatever it is, 'play' to the mood and don't fight it. Context is everything.

7 What is the mood on the day?

- The worst mistake any of us makes is to judge everything to precision except, as actors would put it, 'the smell of the audience on the night'. Before you start presenting you must judge how people are. If they are edgy and unresponsive – maybe they've had a bad car journey or a star team player has had a row before leaving home – sense it and give them all time to settle.

- Perfect performance is not about perfection. What a coup for Neville Coghill and for Oxford – getting Richard Burton at the peak of his career to come up and play Dr Faustus. It was at the height of his affair with Elizabeth Taylor – double coup as she was billed to play Helen of Troy. Richard Burton was no stranger to drink and he drank a lot beneath the dreaming spires. He was rather drunk and he didn't really know his lines – anyone else would have collapsed or been booed off but ... but ... he really knew the meaning, the core essence of the play. It was undoubtedly the definitive Dr Faustus. He performed the emotional meaning, and if the details got blurred well, we can forgive gods like that.

8   How do *you* feel?

> Nerves – you've not conquered them but you have
> controlled them. You are really quite commanding when
> presenting – but suppose you feel ill – you are sweating,
> you have an upset stomach, you feel as if you want to die
> (you are probably dying) , if only the cruel audience knew
> just how you felt. But how you feel physically is not the
> issue. Are you focused and alert and 'up for it' – that's what
> matters. Keep how you feel to yourself. As far as the
> audience is concerned you always feel wonderful.

9   Do you know what the audience feels?

> Get a feel for what it's like being in the audience by going
> and sitting where the audience will sit and getting someone
> else to talk from where you'll be talking.

10 Are you in charge?

- With those management skills you obviously possess you
  can encourage, cajole and tell the people who do coffee,
  tea and lunch to work with you rather than against you.

- Get there early and have chats with the people who are
  often ignored. Whatever happens, at least they will be on
  your side when your presentation starts. A great
  presentation to a small group was sabotaged (slightly but
  badly) by the presenter having a silly and undignified
  disagreement with a waitress who subsequently insisted on
  pointing at him and loudly describing him as 'that idiot over
  there'.

Summary

If you don't know where you are or why you're there, you can't
really know what you are doing. Nor can you do it – whatever it

is – particularly well. I believe that the skill of a brilliant presenter is to know that they've covered the following:

- Why is it happening?
- Where is it happening?
- When is it happening?
- Who will be listening?
- What do they want?
- What do they expect?
- What do they need?
- What's been happening in the world?
- What's been happening in their lives?
- What are their biggest problems right now?

It's hard to stress quite how important getting the 'context' thing right is. Yet most of us are a bit lazy at doing the research and having the conversations ahead of time that help us understand the background factors which could help make a potentially brilliant presentation a failure.

CHAPTER 5

How to write
a brilliant
story

A brilliant story

A recent winner of the UK Whitbread prize for literature is an American, James Shapiro, who claims that he hated Shakespeare at school but is now besotted with him. His book is called *1599* and tells the story of that one year in which William Shakespeare wrote, among other things, *Henry V*, *Julius Caesar*, *As You Like It* and *Hamlet* – not bad for one year's output, not bad stories.

brilliant tip

Be like Shakespeare: a really great story teller

Now, when I talk about the need to 'tell a story' I am not advising you to emulate Shakespeare (although you could do much worse than try) but I am asking you to give me a sense of narrative drive where there is a strong beginning, a coherent middle and a powerful, surprising and memorable ending. In other words, have a tale worth telling.

brilliant tip

Content is king. This is not a book full of sticking plasters that teaches you how to busk it (although I can help you do that too).

Unless you can learn how to create a good and interesting story it is unlikely you will ever be a very good presenter. The starting point is to get to work on what you want to say, your key message – or, as I prefer to put it, your 'story'.

Death to mission statements and other jargon

As I said earlier, in one of the organisations that I chair I have banned the use of that ghastly phrase 'mission statement' and have insisted it is replaced by 'our story'. I am convinced that this will encourage people away from corporate speak, jargon and bullet points towards simplicity, excitement and common-sense.

The great thing about stories is, after all, that they have something to say.

brilliant do's and don'ts

- Don't start at the beginning. Start by deciding what the 'end' is – what the final point is that you want to make. Everything you do must lead up to this final point – everything.

- Do limit your thinking to the 'rule of three' – in this simple technique you are *never* allowed to use more than three points. Try it and see how powerful it is. For example, there are just three things to say about creating a story – stories are designed to command the attention of the audience; stories are about people, things and events; and all stories are about change. (Ironically, at this point I, of course, immediately break the rule of three by moving through my fourth and on to my fifth point. As you get better at presenting remember that rules can be broken.)

- Do try to summarise the thrust of your story in just a few words. For example, if you say 'This presentation is about our growth, how we've achieved it and what we are going to do next,' this will 'fix' in your mind the journey you are going to take. Many of us find it hard to say exactly where we are going, which probably accounts for the fact that so few of us actually get there.

- Do make your story sound fresh and new – as if it has only just happened, and also as though it has happened to you.

- Do give your audience the setting for the story in graphic terms – time, place, temperature, ambience and so on – hook into people's imaginations. Do you remember those stories that started 'It was a dark and stormy night'?

- Don't be squeamish about cutting out anything in your presentation, however nice you think it is, which doesn't drive the story on.

- Do try to create a simple structure so that the presentational story has an order to it. Something like: 1 This is where we were; 2 This is where we are now; 3 This is where we want to be.

- Don't only speak in the third person. Try to introduce first person experiences and anecdotes. For example, I remember a powerful story I told the Department of Health when I was in advertising and we pitched for a teenage anti-smoking campaign. It was about my niece who was given cigarettes by her mother when she went to parties so that if she felt that she really had to smoke she wasn't put at risk of being given one laced with skunk. This anecdote spoke volumes to ministers and their officials.

A way of thinking about your story is to regard it as the framework around which everything else fits. It's a simple truth that if you haven't got a good, sound story to tell then you haven't got a good presentation.

brilliant tip

If you haven't got a good, sound story to tell then you can't produce a good presentation

Truth is a powerful weapon

We are all impressed by what we rather admiringly call 'true stories'. These are narratives that sound as though they might be fictional – 'you're never going to believe this …' – but are grounded in reality and actually happened.

Anecdote wins hands down in a contest with data when it comes to presentations. The politician who personalises his story with an account of a real event grabs the headlines. Presentations in business will be based, almost by definition, on truth (unless of course you are Enron). How do you turn a liturgy of figures and mission statements (oh dear!) into a narrative, a story that commands attention, inspires belief and, hopefully, takes the business forward?

The advice I've given already should help but if you want to achieve brilliance then you have to go further than simply applying a mechanical process. You'll have to learn how that interaction between story, storyteller and audience works.

Does the story grab the imagination?

Martin Conradi, chief of Showcase, proposed the 'mother test'. First, find a mother – any mother will do – and tell her your story. If she understands it and is interested you are probably on to a winner – if, however, she does neither, start again. Martin might well have suggested the 'small child test' because it is young children who are the most fearless of critics and the most expert in the art of sussing out a good or bad story. But let's go beyond the small child to a stroppy teenager. They are the harshest critics of all. This is a question of, are you telling a story an aggressive critic can understand?

In the golden, youthful era of storytelling, the acid test of a good story is whether or not it inspires – the Harry Potter phenomenon is proof enough of that. In our sophisticated, high-tech world, tales of low-level witchcraft have dazzled a generation or two, or more. It has also shown how many adults have 'childlike' minds – they are none the worse for that either. When *Harry Potter and the Half-Blood Prince* came out it went to the top of the best-seller lists in France and Germany – not the French or German versions (published about eight months later) but in English. Picture the poor young folks in Marseille or Munich reading this 600-page tome slow word by slow word just to get their heads round the story.

Become a story student

Listen to the stories that people tell at work, at home, in the pub – wherever. Work out why some work and some fail. Why some are brilliant and others not. Listen to comedians and watch the news. Become a 'story addict'. Learn what seems to work and then adopt the role of storyteller and finally try to grip the atten tion of your audience through the simplicity, conviction and narrative drive of your performance.

Practise, practise, practise – it takes time but keep at it. And don't forget to try it on your mother, a child or a teenager from hell. Set yourself a 'story test'. Keep on asking yourself if the story you are telling contains the 'brilliant story elements'.

The elements of a great story

It needs to be:

- interesting;
- relevant;
- accurate;
- involving;
- clear;
- well structured;
- memorable; and
- make demands on your audience – you do want them to do something as a result of it don't you?

The best presentations were brilliant stories

Some of the best presentations I've heard have been stories of discovery and learning. Others have been sermons – one of the great art forms of all time where a ten-minute story should be designed to make you laugh and frown, and think and remember on different levels.

But the best I ever heard came from Tony O'Reilly. He was talking to the Marketing Society at the Royal Lancaster Hotel in London about German retailing in 1990. He played the Irish British Lion card brilliantly, talking fluently about rugby, Brendan Behan and drinking stories. As a raconteur this man has it all. He looks good, he's rich, he's famous, he's been a great sportsman and he's very funny. Since then he's got richer – a lot richer – and probably funnier too.

I loved the probably apocryphal story of him at Heinz as a very young man determined to win brownie points for his keenness from a workaholic boss. He'd get in really early – say 6.30am – and be there head down when his boss passed by shortly after 7am. Having established his presence he crept off to a quiet part of the building for an hour's snooze at about 7.15am. That's style. It's also quite sensible.

Great memory hook, but what's the story?

One of the most interesting presentations I ever went to was at M&C Saatchi's Golden Square offices one Sunday where the School of Economic Science put on an event . They had really good speakers at the first session I went to – Sir David Putnam, Professor Paul Robertson (spectacularly brilliant on the effects of Mozart on autistic children) and the actress Emily Watson.

On the second occasion it happened Graham Fink spoke first – now creative director of M&C Saatchi but then founder of a creative business called the Fink Tank. Graham spoke well and without notes but rather nervously. I remember that he showed us some ads, that he also stressed the importance of creativity, asserted that he was very creative (which he is), and that there was a middle-aged lady with her hair done up in a scarf sat on stage knitting and ignoring what was going on around her. She turned out to be Fink's mother. The reason she was there was to capture our attention. She was charming but her presence was only relevant as a memory hook.

Telling it like it is – brilliantly

The late Michael Mayne, former Dean of Westminster followed Graham Fink. He was heavily scripted, and he read it – each word – but every word was pregnant with meaning. He was brilliant in describing the story of how transcendental experiences could be obtained, in virtually equal measure, from great art, great music, great poetry and from spiritual experiences themselves. He read from Milton, played Mozart, described or showed paintings. The whole experience was magical – a cornucopia of pleasures heard, as it were, sitting at the feet of a mightier, albeit humble, human being. I thought Michael was a genius.

Yet when we spoke afterwards he said that he was bemused to be juxtaposed with Mr Fink, saying he hadn't understood what he'd been talking about or why everyone had seemed to take him so seriously. I explained that as an ex-adman I could speak with authority on the subject – that ads had their place, that ads were indeed fine but flippant by nature because they were transient and that Shakespeare, Mozart, Rembrandt and God might prove to be just a touch more timeless!

Summary

Most of us are much better at telling stories than we think. These stories don't have to be original (none of Shakespeare's were) but they have to be good, solid, structured and told well. Storytellers give themselves time and space and have good material. Take the Bible. Full of great stories. Take Milton's *Paradise Lost*; a great story. Or Philip Pulman's Dark Materials series – Milton reincarnated.

Another great storyteller is Tom Peters whose power of delivery may be a greater factor in his success than his ability to dissect a management situation. Yet he tells power story after power story compellingly. I also love his own story – imagine, he said, your own gravestone. What he wants on his is 'Tom Peters – he was a player'. Perfect.

I heard him in Amsterdam some time ago and I thought he was great. He made brilliant use of anecdote and of his vivid experiences in companies such as South Western Airlines. It was, incidentally, Herb Kelleher, the one time chief of South Western, who uttered the down-to-earth immortal line, devoid of jargon: 'Yeah we have a strategy at South Western – we do things.' So the next time you're preparing for a presentation steal this directness – 'Yeah I'm going to do a presentation – I have a story to tell.'

Remember, next time you present, that if you haven't got a story then you haven't got a presentation. So before you start say to yourself . . . 'Oh boy, yes . . . do I have a story to tell!'

CHAPTER 6

How to give your story colour

There are more and more good presenters out there today. Their 'presenting' is earning them promotion and jobs. They are developing their careers whilst they are on stage. While they may have mastered many aspects of presenting, real competitive edge can only be gained by that unusual ability to give your story and your presentation a splash of colour.

A nearly brilliant presentation in the making

Suppose you have a good story that withstands the pressure of interrogation and that obeys all the tenets of presenting:

- It is relevant to your audience.
- It has a clear message.
- You applied the 'less is more' rule ruthlessly to the point that it is now incredibly cryptic.
- It is ten minutes long even though they asked you to give them half an hour.
- It has no detours, no irrelevance, no shades of anything but grey.

In short, it has a great framework and is likely to be as dull as tap water – totally clear with just a faint back taste of urine (well, this presentation sounds as though it has been through about thirty audiences already).

Anyone could do this – even a Dalek. Actually a Dalek might do it better.

A bare presentation is like bare walls

This chapter is about helping to put the intellectual ornaments and rhetorical colouring into your simple story – the stuff that will turn it from being a plot line into a narrative that engages the audience's mind. Something with shades of colour and emphasis. Something with highlights and lowlights with solid logic and emotional intelligence, which has a certainty of where it is heading, what its ultimate destination will be but which has surprises and interesting detours en route.

brilliant tip

The stuff that transforms a bare plot line into a narrative that engages the audience's mind is colour and atmosphere

So how do you find these embellishments? As Dylan Thomas said, 'Let's start at the beginning.'

brilliant do's and don'ts

● Do work at breakfast time. Read as many papers as you can. Focus on the *Financial Times*, *The Times* and the *Sun*. But always read *The Week* and *Private Eye* too. Snip out any good stories. One of the things that freshens any story is something contemporary, something that's just happened, something recent that demonstrates a point you want to make. Be ruthless in choosing a story that makes you look up to date – best of all, of course, is the statement of the type 'this appeared in today's *FT* – What do you make of it? Let me make just three points about it …'

There's something about 'morning fresh' that is captivating. It positions you as an on-the-ball person.

- Do read the most brilliant management books. You have no choice as an aspiring 'big-time-brilliant presenter' but to be an avid consumer of the key, current management books – from Tom Peters to Jack Welch, Jim Collins to Patrick Lencioni, Michael Heppell through to a much longer list. These are people who will give you insights, thoughts or who will simply give you amazing slides. You don't have to read all these cover to cover of course – just learn to be a great scanner. Look for the big thought or quote – and keep one eye open for a big idea.

- Do keep a look out for big pictures. These are all around us but we'd seldom either think or have the courage to use them – pictures of the World Cup or the Ryder Cup or the Tsunami in Thailand or fires in Los Angeles or the Olympics in Beijing or – the list is endless. Some will be corny and some contemporary. Some will be pictures you've seen before – the Laughing Cavalier, the Scream, the Mona Lisa, Picasso's Guernica, Hurst's Sheep, Tracy Emin's Bed. Look out for the great news pictures, especially recent ones that will resonate with your audience. Also look out for visual treats in the papers – study the *Financial Times* which, at its best, does some awesome design work with financial results.

There is nothing more colourful and exciting than to be taken on a big adventurous presentational journey.

- Don't take things for granted. Curiosity might have killed the cat but, as sure as anything, it makes a business presentation sing. Curiosity delivers quirky insights, it is the lead-in to discovering the unusual, the story or fact that can captivate an audience. Curiosity's currency is the line made famous by Michael Caine, 'And not many people know that.' Someone asked me what I mean by 'being curious'. What I mean is keeping your eyes open and seeing what's changed, what's stayed the same, what's died, what's been born, what's been relaunched.

Become a question machine and an accumulator of oddball stories. Read *Google Zeitgeist*. Look. Listen. Question.

- Do keep a 'brilliant ideas' book beside you. You have to keep a book in which the great quotes and insights you gather are kept. Not because you are a train spotter who has to write everything down but because you never know when they may be useful in fleshing out a presentation. For example, you are talking about the importance of speed in business today – Mario Andretti, the great Formula One driver, said: 'If you're in control you aren't going fast enough.' Now that's similar to the comment made to the British ice skating champion Robin Cousins who was told that he wasn't going to make it because 'he didn't skate to fall'. Consider both of these quotes and what they mean. Could you do a presentation just focusing on these two quotes? Or suppose there's been a corporate marriage. I love this one, by Anthony Hilton in the *Evening Standard* writing on takeovers and mergers: 'The lunch comes immediately; the bill comes later.'

- Don't have dull slides. Jack Welch tells stories of how he and his colleagues spent hours trying to refine just one chart that encapsulated a whole strategic thought. Finding a way of talking about, say, a new people-strategy may be as arid as the Sahara when expressed in bullet points but in contrasting the two shapes or – if your people are really clever – morphing from a triangle (normal structure) to say a circle (twenty-first century structure) may say more things more quickly and more clearly than you can imagine.

  Besides which, interesting material and visual material can be more interesting for you to talk to. Too many words on screen can slow you down.

- Don't underestimate the importance of agendas. They are the key to expectation but ironically most people regard the agenda as a necessary extra that sits rather drably in the 'conference housekeeping drawer'. But how would you feel about a restaurant with a scruffy menu? Your agenda *is* your menu. Treat it as the way of previewing how the meeting is going to be – serious and data filled, fun and innovative, about people, about the future or a review of the past. It's the dustcover to the book you are going to launch so treat it with great respect and produce something that looks colourful, well-thought out, attention-getting and important. At recent meetings we've had laminated agendas, pocket-sized agendas, bookmark agendas – anything that takes you from the prosaic.

The next one will be circular, or we might print it on an inflatable. Well that would be a great way of doing an agenda for a global conference.

- Don't forget take-aways. These are reminders of the event – at analysts' meetings you need presentation printouts on which they can make their copious notes. But these represent a small part of all the meetings and presentations that most people have to do. What every presentation needs is an elegant follow-up, and I love what Martin Conradi at Showcase invented – he calls them 'lunch-books'. They are called this because they are ring bound, A5 and easy to handle so you can use them while having lunch without knocking the water over or anything else. They contain the slides and as many appendices as are necessary.

  A good takeaway puts the gloss on a great presentation. Perhaps more importantly it easily follows things up and you can turn a one-off audience into a lifelong network.

- Do remember the power of the 'money shot'. There is that moment in every Bond film that has people sitting on the edge of their seats – the one that everyone tells their friends about: 'So-so movie but that bit where they go over the glacier on a snowmobile is incredible'. In the same way with presentations we are looking for charismatically memorable effects. Now these are not *always* appropriate, especially with small audiences where pyrotechnics will seem superfluous. But for larger audiences you need not only that killer slide but also that moment of drama – maybe borrowed from a favourite film. Maybe it's animation. We did a fairly corny but very effective 'tipping point' animation recently using a seesaw that is incredibly hard to move until – whoops – suddenly it tips and all else follows. Corny but memorable. Look to have a moment in your presentation you are looking forward to presenting – a moment to remember.

- Always involve the audience. I was asked by a client recently how real audience involvement could be achieved at a relatively small seminar. When I said 'Well, you could start by giving them sweets,' I think she thought I'd gone mad. Of course, what I was suggesting was interaction. Sweets, chocolates – anything like that would do – sampling drinks if it's relevant. Sampling an ordinary Bordeaux and a great New World wine both selling at the same price is a great way of starting a presentation or a debate on the new order and how things are changing today. To make it really interesting you could include Great Wall wine from China too – old world, new world, next world. Now that's a scary presentation to which I really want to come. Give them ice cream if it's hot and lead a debate on climate change – then do your presentation but with interruptions and questions encouraged as you go along. Take risks, be imaginative, run polls on issues, do it electronically on screen. It creates amazing tensions and excitements and, for some reason, we all seem to love scores. Do live interviews – get people up on stage with you – pass microphones around the audience.

● Become a compere not just a presenter.

These are the 'big tips' but I also want you and your team to think about how you can become more colourful and exciting. How you can keep on trying to achieve brilliant effects.

● Be fresh. Think of every presentation as a new one, not one that is re-hashed. A presentation will nearly always be enhanced by individualised splashes of colour because it will appear to be 'freshly cooked', as opposed to being ready prepared in some presentation factory or, worse still, a congealed leftover from a previous meeting.

● Think creatively about your presentation. We live in a world of increasing sophistication. Most of us are processing more and more arcane pieces of information. They used to say that information is power. This may be true for Google, but for the rest of us clarity of thought and creativity are what are really powerful. Information is merely there to be used. So use it – use it to intrigue and to educate; use it to make your presentations more fun and more lively.

- Thinking on your feet is colourful in itself. One of the most exciting presentations I ever saw that was crammed with colour was by Rosabeth Moss Kanter who ran a masterclass in strategy at the London Business School. Her flashes of colour were all intellectual but not everyone is as clever as she is.

- Nearly too late. And the most difficult I have done myself was to a roomful of Chinese, Russians and Iranians in Shenzen at the Global Holography Conference. I had two simultaneous translators sitting in what looked like a Tardis at the end of the room, along with 300 slides operated by a green-faced (because she felt so sick with nerves) Chinese girl – an MA from Warwick University as I discovered – who confessed, just before we embarked on the three-hour talk, that she had never done this before but she did brilliantly – one small flaw in 300 slides (and, hey, that's a top six sigma score.) There was no technical run through – the Chinese are not used to such things. When I discovered this my language was quite colourful too. This was a classic example of a cultural difference in a way of working. They think it's 'just in time'; we think it's 'nearly too late'.

brilliant tip

It's clarity of thought and creativity that is really powerful: information is merely a tool to be used

brilliant tip

Do not aim to be ordinary. Good enough is no good. Brilliant is the target

Summary

The moral is to ask these questions of yourself and your team at that first critical meeting, when you are writing the brief for your presentation:

- This is going to be brilliant. Can we remember that whatever we are doing?
- How do we make this presentation totally different, one that is quite different from expectation?
- How do we give it a real extra wow factor?
- How do we, as a team, find those splashes of colour, extraordinary effects that will have the audience saying 'That was a very good story – but wasn't it amazingly interesting and memorable too'?

CHAPTER 7

How to illustrate your presentation

Opera is narrative brought to life by music. There is a powerful simplicity to many operatic stories but it's the music that makes it fly. Great visual aids, like the music in opera, can take your rhetoric and your argument to a higher level than if you simply rely on the spoken word. Some people I know work whilst playing opera. The one thing opera is not is understated. Nor should you be as a presenter.

Think of slides as your music

Even if you don't actually have any slides, don't for one moment imagine that you are doing an un-illustrated presentation – if you have no visual aids you have made a decision to make *you yourself* the illustration. How you look, what you wear and the way you behave will have even more importance than normal.

Bad slides slow you down

Curiously, many people seem to regard slides as a mere adjunct to a presentation – a kind of necessary evil. Good and sharp visuals help to drive a presentation, making it easier to understand and more compelling than if there were none, but poor visuals slow everything down – like trying to drive with the handbrake on.

brilliant tip

Poor visuals slow everything down – like trying to drive with the handbrake on

Equally, while anyone can cobble themselves together a half decent, conventional kind of presentation, many are fettered by bullet points – the presentational equivalent of sleeping policemen.

Professional slides help

On the other hand, a really skilled operator can, with experience, make a PowerPoint presentation look wonderful. I used to work in advertising and there was one piece of advice I consistently gave clients: 'Don't try to do your own advertising.' As with DIY surgery, the result will not necessarily be what you would wish.

By the same token, make sure that you get trained and experienced people to finish off your visuals if you want them to have great impact. *Don't try to do them yourself – unless, of course, the casual, amateur look is something you want to project.*

Professorial vagueness has its place

Interestingly, many academics seem to be happiest with scratched, out of order and apparently frequently changed overheads. These create a very public denunciation of style. So far as they are concerned they are saying that substance and work in progress is all that matters. Do we imagine that Newton would have had a very snazzy presentation with gorgeous shots of apples? Or would it have been an old envelope? Or more like the erratic genius Robin Hankey, whom I knew at Oxford and who wrote his essays from west to east and then turned the paper round 90 degrees and carried on writing north to south over the previous text?

We return to scrutiny of the context of a presentation if we want to decide on the most appropriate visual techniques and the amount of money we want to spend.

Less is more

In general, I advocate a 'less is more' approach. Keep the number of slides down to perhaps one a minute. Go for maximum focus and few words. Consider animation. Include video if you can – talking, for instance, about a retail outlet while watching a possibly speeded up video of it can work much more powerfully than looking at a sales graph. Consider big, bold, single word slides such as:

FOCUS

You have to concede it gets your attention.

A favourite idea of mine involved a presentation for a firm of accountants when we wanted to talk about the benefits of partnership – how working together, client and accountant, could achieve synergistic benefits. This was the slide that did that:

$$2 + 2 = 5$$

So how do you set about achieving this?

---

brilliant do's and don'ts

- Do know what you are saying, to whom and what you want to achieve. Showing pictures of storm troopers with the slogan 'Let's go get 'em' may not be that helpful in a presentation about partnership and stakeholder relationships. The pictures have to illustrate the story you are telling, not something else.

- Do know first of all how many there are in the audience, how big the hall is, how smart and attuned an audience you have, whether there are language difficulties (more of this later). Your slides need more impact the bigger the hall.

- Don't be too corporate. Do be you. I have a personal antipathy to corporate templates, which nearly always swamp the presenter's good intentions in 'corporate porridge'. Yet I am a lifelong advocate of brand values. I am a passionate fan of Heinz with whom I've worked on many projects over the years. You don't need to slam 'HJ Heinz' at the bottom of every slide with bullets shaped like the famous keystone to make it look like a Heinz presentation. Indeed, the best presentation I ever saw from them was done smartly without such constraints and yet it breathed that sense of 'there's no taste like Heinz' in a way that a more mechanistic offering could never have done. If you are not doing a corporate but more a personal presentation, decide in a focused – almost a feminine – way on your 'look'. This involves font, colours, feel and style. There is a later chapter in this book that warns against using exotic and mysterious fonts in case in the transportation of a presentation from one computer to another the font is not recognised. I discovered such a font recently which, for obvious reasons, looked good to me on my computer – it is called 'Poor Richard' and here's how it appeared on another PC: ꙮ℩℮⬛℮𝒶☜◯⌘⬛!

Avoid indulgences such as 'Poor Richard' like the plague – life is hard enough without being a presentational punk.

- You do need toys. Not everything visual has to appear on a screen. Assuming that it was relevant, you might put a packet of jelly beans on the seat of every member of the audience, or a specially created agenda – or if you're talking about innovation and you want to explore that wow factor why not put a 'WOW' card on every seat for the audience to wave whenever they feel a wow moment (just as cricket spectators wave big 4s when a boundary is scored). Nick Horswell, ex-colleague and founder of the media company PHD, once did a presentation which climaxed (I'm not entirely sure that is the right word) in his walking off stage trouserless from behind the lectern having walked on stage fully trousered. I'm not sure how he did it, undoing his pants and still giving a decent presentation, but he did. Suffice it to say that trousers-down Horswell also brought the house down.

● Don't hang back. Be real. if you are talking about a product, work out how to make the product the 'hero'. Years ago I met Jilly Cooper, before she became a super star writer. I was a very young, impressionable and a very enthusiastic advertising executive working on a new account, Jeyes, one of whose products was a loo cleaner called Sanilav. I carefully emptied the loo cleaner into a Dartington glass tumbler where it fizzed bluely and angrily. Jilly mused that I looked like a thirsty man about to drink a gin and tonic and that it must be really good. I remember feeling so strongly that there had never been a better, bluer loo cleaner. I was so happy to be promoting it. The lesson is, wherever you can, use and dramatise products. Pass them round. Make people see them close up, touch them and taste them. Don't just let them sit there lifeless on a screen.

● Enjoy doing your slides. Think of things from the audience's point of view. Think about how to get them on your side, about colour, about simple points. Can you get pictures of any of your audience on screen? Or of the buyer of your product at Tesco? Something that speaks to your audience. If you think of this as hard work and boring it will show.

● Don't forget – a picture is worth 10,000 words. But it has to be the right picture. If a presenter is talking about, say, productivity and a picture of a carrot appears on the screen then the audience is likely to be baffled. I recently did a presentation in China which, given the language issues, had to be predominantly visual. The key point is, of course, that finding great visuals that begin to tell a story is very, very time consuming. I and three researchers spent an indecently long time scouring the web to find exactly what I wanted.

- Do go for the tour de force. This is the sort of thing the ever-brilliant Richard Eyres, now a non-executive director at the Guardian Media Group, has used in presentations. I've seen him do a great presentation in which he talked, among other things, about the creation of the Capital Radio website (it had to be 'not leading edge or even cutting edge – it had to be bleeding edge' according to the designers). An executive from Pearson, as I recall hearing it told to me, did a very energetic presentation with a new slide every seven seconds or so. 'Don't do it' begged the producers. But he did. And I'm told it was a complete wow. Sometimes you have to go for it.

- Don't make it all the same. What can look like a neat, clear presentation as a booklet to be taken away can be the equivalent of a monotonic drone presented on the big screen. Presentation is theatre ... with pauses ... with lows and highs, fast bits and slooowwweeerr bits. The visual impact of your presentation can catapult you to the heights or, if it's boring, act like the deadweight of a sea anchor.

- Do compile a brief in cryptic words and pictures. Your designer can't really be expected to read your script and immediately understand what you are trying to achieve. So get a few A5 sheets and create a series of simplistic charts with a thick felt tip pen. This is a Showcase trick to stop you putting too many words on a slide. No more than ten words to a slide is ideal – the best creative directors in advertising used to claim no poster should have more than six words, so check some of today's posters. See how you get on being this reductive. Then try it again seeing if you can spot opportunities for some visual fun. Then again to see if the slides tell your story. If you need special emphasis then indicate where this is. Now you are ready to brief your presentation designer.

Why people avoid slides

There are many reasons why many presenters are nervous of slides.

- Except when they were under five, most people have always been used to verbal and written communication, not visual communication.

- They wouldn't know a good piece of visual communication if it bit them on the leg.

- The moment something goes on a slide, technology gets involved and anything can happen.

- It isn't just technology, it's about control. Some people say: 'I'd rather have average PowerPoint slides I've done myself that I can change at the last minute.' I know what they mean but they don't really, really mean it? Do they? Not really. Because mediocre is not what an aspiring brilliant presenter wants to be.

---

brilliant example

A guy at Royal Bank of Scotland Insurance had rehearsed his big set piece presentation, which was at a foreign location. He'd have scored A+ for preparation. But he went up on stage and the people running the show managed to let their computer go down. Blank screen – crisis! Fortunately he was able to chill out and stay calm. They rebooted and off he went again – 'whew!' Do your knees feel weak? Mine do. I hate technology except when it goes right when I really love it.

It's all a bit like former US president Gerald Ford, of whom it was said he couldn't walk and chew gum at the same time. You have a lot to do and a lot to remember – you have your nerves to conquer, your words to say, things to remember and slides to pay attention to – something's going to crash. Don't laugh at that poor president – maybe he had a point.

Possibly the worst presentation – but there are so many, OK one of the worst I ever saw – was when I saw a nervous ad man go off at pace pressing his own slide button. This was before the age of computers and he managed to go the wrong way, so the final slide came up first and his 'Welcome' slide came up last. The slides and his words bore no relation to each other. Having been told never to look behind you at the screen he didn't, and so had no idea what was going on. There were quiet mutterings among the audience, and then laughter which he thought was at a joke and this just encouraged him the more. He speeded up – he shouted 'Sales will grow' to the accompaniment of a half-dressed girl lying on the bonnet of a car with the headline 'Big Engines are a Turn On'. People in the audience stood up and shouted. He just got louder and faster. Someone approached the stage and tried to help but the presenter resisted exclaiming 'I shall have my say.'

Whether or not you use slides consider the following:

- You are in trouble if you don't find out if those before and after you are using them. An audience that has just experienced half an hour of blazing visual pyrotechnics will feel it odd trying to adjust to you standing there with a blank screen. Don't you care? Didn't you have time to produce any slides? Do you prefer mono as opposed to stereo or even 3D presentations? You'll have to be really good to overcome the poor no-slide-impression you'll create.

- If you don't use slides then *you* are the visual. Everyone will look at you intently, so you'd better be very interesting or very important. Or else exciting – no need for handstands, but do deliver an interesting mix of pitch, pace and movement.

- You can hide behind the lectern but then they will focus on your face. This scenario could be very dull unless your content and delivery are riveting and you have a great voice. It will help to keep things very brief – it is ill-advised for any stand-up speech without slides, however good it is, to last for more than ten minutes.

● If you do use slides then understand that a dramatic change in the presentational dynamic is achieved. You have stopped being the star – you are now the voice-over. No one is looking at you – they are staring at the screen. And if you care about your appearance then care about your slides – when the audience looks at them they are assessing you.

● Poor slides are the presentational equivalent of scuffed shoes, a dirty crumpled shirt and a curry-stained tie.

brilliant tip

If you care about your appearance then you should care about your slides

Summary

Are you allowed to be boring? In a word, no. But you are allowed to set up and control a PowerPoint presentation yourself and deliver it sparingly to small audiences provided that you:

● have very few slides;

● use very big words;

● include quotes (these are always good);

● speak interestingly and excitedly to them.

Quite simply, life is too short for boring presentations, boring ads or boring people. We live in a post-boring world, one in which stand-up presentations are the norm. The standards are rising. What was considered to be a brilliant presentation twenty years ago is probably merely good by today's standards.

The one element that has really come on over the years is visual design. All kinds of tricks are possible in this wonderful age of special effects. Realise that your slides complement your voice and if you really seek brilliance, pay attention to them and their production. Let the 'visual voice' have space and time for expression. Done well, it will add a dramatic dimension to the other brilliant aspects of your presentations.

CHAPTER 8

Performance

How you put yourself across to your audience is the key. No, you are not expected to be a professional performer but you are expected to perform. You are expected to put on a bit of a show because that's what presentations need – a bit of underlining, a bit of *drama*, a bit of *swagger*. Remember that the audience *wants* you to wow them. Don't let them down.

What acting can do

Dustin Hoffman takes his job very seriously. When he was in *Marathon Man* he had to appear exhausted in one scene. Ever the perfectionist, he stayed up all night and arrived on the set the next day white, puffy eyed and knackered. Laurence Olivier surveyed him in amusement: 'Why don't you try acting dear boy? It's so much easier.'

In praise of work – in praise of America

While Britain was creating Raffles, the Americans were creating Rockefellers. While Britain was defending an empire they were building an economy. They worked incredibly hard – they still do. They don't dream the 'American dream' – they create it brick by brick. Their success is founded on an astonishing attention to detail. Whenever you hear people knock the USA as many do, remember their work ethic.

So it was with Al Pacino when he performed Shakespeare's *Richard III*. Pacino gathered the cast around and dissected the text word by word, examining meaning and motive until it became clearer and clearer what was going on. Shakespeare, he told his exhausted fellow thespians, wasn't casual or sloppy. If a word was there, it was there for a reason.

So it is with presenting – if a word is there it must be there for a reason. Getting it right will only be achieved by rigorous questioning and a refusal to stop until you get to the bottom of an issue. I recommend such rigour to you in preparing a presentation. If you work in an American company you will find that exhaustive examination of every word and nuance is commonplace.

Illogical arguments show up in a presentation

The question is 'Does the argument hold water?' *not* 'Is this good rhetoric?' Don't be sloppy in building an argument and in creating the logic of your story. At least one acid test of building a credible presentation lies in the practice of constantly interrogating the logic and the flow.

Don't go to bed until you've cracked it. Remember *Marathon Man*. Toyota created 'the five whys' as their process of inquisition whereby any proposal was intellectually tortured until it confessed to its weakness, or survived through the strength of its truth, convictions and logic. For example, suppose that a young executive has a proposal for his company to launch a range of premium organic chilled meals. His boss is sceptical.

● **Why** are you making this proposal when our resources are already overstretched?

    Because research shows there's a big gap in the market for this concept, and it is very high margin so there's an incremental volume and profit opportunity. And I'll put in extra time myself to make sure it gets done. The resource issue is down to me and my time.

- **Why** is no one else in this sector – doesn't this suggest there may be something they know that we don't?

  Because it's hard to get the product right, because there's a difficult trade sell to do (but I know we can do this) and because no one else has our organic credentials so competitors are wisely steering clear. Anyway, I think we're a bit smarter than them.

- **Why** do you think that we can overcome trade antipathy, which you concede is a problem, and also live with a potential private label offering? If Tesco were to agree with your market diagnosis they could simply do it themselves – and probably would.

  Because if we can get Tesco to stock, in addition to the easier targets like Sainsbury and Waitrose – and I think we can because the taste tests on our product are exceptional – then the organic story plus our pricing makes this a must-stock range. Tesco may do a Finest range but that would be no big deal.

- **Why** should we do this and run the risk of cannibalising our successful, but static and under margin-pressure, non-organic offering?

  Because it's all down to positioning isn't it? If we launch head to head against ourselves then you have a strong point, but if we aim more upmarket and go for people organically predisposed and avoid recipe duplication, then we should be OK.

- **Why** would you want to put your career on the line now, just when you are in line for promotion? You see, if this fails to hit plan your life here is over, and I doubt if any of our competitors would be impressed either. Will you think about that?

That's a very strong point boss and very well made. Can I go away and have a think about it? What sort of promotion did you actually have in mind by the way?

Why? Why?? Why??? Why???? Why?????

This technique will usually find the weak point in any argument, position or presentation. Try it on the argument for your next presentation. Through laziness or because we can't quite make the argument compute, most of us make jumps in our logic, bury issues that don't suit the argument or, if we are politicians, sometimes fib. Sometimes, we even tell really big porkies just to get a brilliant presentation away – sometimes, 2 + 2 = 5 because we can't be bothered to do the simple arithmetic.

brilliant tip

Sometimes we're tempted to tell really big porkies just to get our presentation flying

A strong argument helps you feel confident

Your performance deserves a strong, bulletproof argument (as opposed to just bullet points). Not only will it always be better if it has this, it will also be easier to perform – no more butterflies about being destroyed by questions because of corrupt logic.

So let's consider the ways in which performance can be advanced so that you stand out as a presenter. At this stage there will be those among you who say that you hate acting. If this is the case there is little I can do for you. But remember, corporate life nowadays involves a degree of acting.

⚡ brilliant do's and don'ts

- Do be yourself (just a bigger you). David Abbott, one of the legendary advertising figures of the twentieth century, spoke with contempt of people going into presentation-speak, hunched up, glazed eyes, Dalek-voiced and didactic. There's no need for that. Just do a bit of self-examination – of the way you look, the way you move, the way you sound and your very presence. This is a hard thing to pin down but there are people who have authority and those who don't – those who inspire trust and those who don't. Take what you have and make a vow to lift yourself up two or three levels. Be bigger. Impose. But don't be someone else. Especially don't be Mr Hectoring.

- Do work on your voice. This is your biggest asset – or liability. For most audiences it's all that exists of you when you give a 'whiz bang' slide presentation. How do you feel about your voice? Personally, I like and I lean on mine. It sounds deep and strong and it gives me confidence – I can play with its range and pace. When it isn't quite there, through a cold or a surprise attack of nerves, my sense of self-belief begins to flutter. Your voice is as important to you as a presenter as your putting stroke is to you as a golfer – so look after it. Record yourself and listen to yourself. Work with a coach if necessary – and it probably is. Someone who slows you down, who makes you speak in lower bass tones. Look at what Sir Gordon Reece managed to do for Margaret Thatcher – she was transformed from a Finchley housewife politician who, as education minister, stopped school milk ('Margaret Thatcher – school milk snatcher') to a world statesperson who spoke with gravitas and passion. The late Edward Heath had voice coaching with the same result – a statesmanlike burr.

- Do work on how you look. Of course you need help, how can you work this out yourself? Get advice on how to dress – for women, a well-cut trouser suit always looks powerful and modern; for men, a dark suit with a white or light blue shirt and no tie (though you can if you want). Slight sun tan – no workaholic you – always better without glasses but if you do wear them have enough pairs to give a range of impressions from severe to magisterial, from mischievous to intellectual. Do not let anyone, however well intentioned, make you wear anything or have a look that makes you feel awkward. The whole point about this is to make you feel better about yourself – you are the star. You need to think and feel that you look your best to be your best.

● Do you have stage presence? Look around you as you go on stage – the bigger the stage, the bigger the look and the bigger the sweep of your gaze. Walk on with a straight back. However you really feel, look as though you are glad to be there – it's worth repeating that, look as though you are glad to be there. Smile and say 'Ha!' under your breath – especially under your breath if you are miked-up – it will animate your face. If it's a smaller event, simply try to be engaged and interested in what is going on and when you start or stand up to speak make eye contact with a few people and think 'Hey, I really like these people.' It's amazing how this communicates to an audience. The number of times I've seen ill-at-ease, shifty, grumpy or even downright hostile speakers is legion. Try to imagine that the people out there have loads of money and that they are going to give some to you, but only if you look cheerful and glad to be with them. Stage presence is like sex appeal – some people have it naturally, some acquire it. Whenever Marilyn Monroe stepped into a room everyone stopped and noticed – and that wasn't just because she had big boobs.

● Do you radiate self-belief? As someone once said to me, 'You have to believe what you are saying even if you don't believe it.' What is it that marks out the brilliant presenter? The best presenters in the advertising business tend to be shameless showmen. 'Shameless' is such a great word – say it to yourself next time you walk up on stage, 'Hey I feel totally shameless today', and see what happens. All you have to do is radiate confidence and a conviction about your subject. Lord Denning, one of the more formidable orators of the twentieth century and a fine lawyer, recalled his pupil master saying to him: 'People pay us for our certainty, not for our doubts.'

● Don't talk in jargon. Something about standing up in public and talking has always (once I conquered my nerves) made me giggle. And in truth many presentations are absurd, especially in a world where jargon is rife. A few years ago someone invented 'bullshit bingo' – a game in which you drew a box within which were 36 squares. Each square contained a piece of management jargon – going forward, strategic, focus, blue sky, global, scale-up, benchmarking, culture, ratio, downsizing, outsourcing and so on. The game was to mark off each loathsome word as it occurred and if a vertical or horizontal line was filled then the lucky winner leapt to their feet shouting 'bullshit'. Avoid all jargon, speak English – in short sentences with short words. And remember that the way a script is written bears no relation to normal writing – it should have short sentences, big type; it should be fast . . . conversational . . . bold.

- Don't avoid being dramatic. You know where you are, why and to whom you are talking. You have a good, simple, strong story and the logic is sound and bombproof. The slides are coming along nicely. Yet you need to impart some surprise or 'oomph' into it at, say, two points so that you stand out from your colleagues (in other words your competitors) and so that the audience remembers your message. Vivid recollections of mine focus on disasters – the slide projector catching fire with the slides melting in front of us . . . 'why we shall succeed' dripping into the reproachful word 'succ', which slowly blackened and disappeared; the slides that had been fed in back to front making it look as though the presentation was in an eastern European language. Think of what you most want your audience to remember and then brainstorm a solution that dramatises the point. It could be a huge word on the screen, a piece of animation or video or soundtrack, a great quote – or you could remove your jacket, tie and shoes saying 'this is about removing excess cost and baggage'. Whatever. It's about finding just one moment when you go for a bit of dramatic emphasis.

- Don't be too mechanical: breathe life into your stuff. On the road to brilliance you have to learn to make what you say attention-grabbing and interesting. When you stand up, you have to look as though you care. You have to breathe life into the case you are making. You have to be passionate for your cause. You have to be (and be seen to be) glad to be doing your presentation. I was recently at an event celebrating an Afruca anniversary (Africans Unite Against Child Abuse). While there, I reflected how much better the Africans were at demonstrating passion, sincerity and involvement. The reason, I suspect, that so few leaders currently come from the UK is that we are hopeless at being extrovert – unlike the South Africans, Zimbabweans, Australians, Americans, French, Italians. So when you get up there give it some 'welly'. Be animated – look and sound *dynamic*.

- Don't be shy: learn some Shakespeare and declaim. Or, it could be Keats, Shelley, T.S. Eliot or Roger McGough – anyone you like. Just learn it and then try saying it out loud – in the bathroom to start with, then outside. Raise your voice and let go with exaggerated theatricality. Enjoy yourself. All I want is for you to be in total control of the content so that you can focus on delivery. For example, imagine reciting *Ode to a Nightingale* to a child, your parents, an old lady, someone dying, a lover, in a large church to two hundred people, in a sitting room to twelve people. The exercise is in learning, delivering the same thing in different contexts and exploring your own range of expression. Enjoy!

- Practise, practise, practise. You will need technical run-throughs and you will need to know your material well. Also, the situation may be changing, which means you may have to be nimble-footed enough to change parts of your presentation at the last moment. But most of all you must leave yourself time to explore performance – to work on pace, on pauses, on the louder and on the softer bits. Don't imagine that any good performance you've ever seen wasn't very well practised. Practise alone so you get used to your own voice. Don't do what some have attempted – editing and moving material around while performing. This is nerve-racking for technicians and rotten for the performance – what you have when you start is what you go with. Do at least two trial runs – the first is what I'd call a 'walk-through', just to make sure all the elements sit together; then a 'run-through' which is a rehearsal with feeling. Mark up your script with cryptic notes and dream the performance in slow motion. Have a plan B – there could be a power cut or a fire, maybe hardly anyone turns up, maybe you are the only speaker standing because of dodgy pasta at dinner that you alone missed because you were rehearsing. There is no substitute for maximising your chance of success through practice.

brilliant tip

If you're on stage we have no place for the Quiet Man. Aim for a power performance with loads of feeling and confidence

Summary

A bit of theatricality is vital if you want to be brilliant. You are not there to talk or to read a script – you are there to command attention and convince. Tom Peters and Jim Collins have been engaged in an energetic debate about styles of leadership. The former advocates charismatic, noisy, female and iconoclastic; the latter is all for quiet, reserved, process-driven, short-term versus long-term.

Well, we don't have a 'long term' any more – we have *now*. And if you're on stage we have no place for the Quiet Man – remember the Ian Duncan Smith debacle? Aim for a powerful performance with lots of feeling and loads of confidence.

CHAPTER 9

I've got the power

PowerPoint is regarded as a critical and brilliant tool by many presenters. Yet opinion about it is polarised – I regard it as a brilliantly useful tool that focuses thinking and enables you to produce, at the least, easy-to-assimilate handouts and, at best, swinging slides. Even so, it's just a tool. This chapter is more about process than anything else. But do remember that if you want the best from your career-shaping presentation then create a relationship with a professional slide designer and marvel at the difference you get, between, as it were, your fast food and their cordon bleu.

The power of PowerPoint

There are, we're told thirty million PowerPoint presentations done every day – or, if you prefer, 350 PowerPoint presentations start every second. That's a thousand since I started typing this sentence (I'm a slow typist). Around eleven billion presentations a year are hitting the population – that means there are about twice as many PowerPoint presentations a year as there are people on the planet. There are PowerPoint presentations everywhere.

Radical mind day and night all the time . . . Maniac brainiac winning the game (from 'I've Got the Power', by Snap)

I love PowerPoint because it is one of the newest persuasion tools around – it's certainly maniac but it can be 'brainiac' too.

It started in Silicon Valley – a man called Bob Gaskins, with a doctorate from Berkeley had the idea. He developed it with Dennis Austen at a company called Forethought. PowerPoint 1 was designed for Apple Macs in black and white, followed quickly by a colour version. They were bought up by Microsoft at the end of a maniac year for $14 million. Bob must have thought 1987 was full of Christmases. I wonder what he thinks now.

Pluses and minuses

The software has its advantages:

- It makes people begin to think visually.
- It's great for consistency – leading to a coherent, corporate feel.
- It can create greater memorability of the presentation as a whole.

However, it has weaknesses too:

- It is very easy to manipulate, which generally leads to too many charts.
- Too much time is wasted on tweaking.
- PowerPoint presentations are generally ugly because people are not trained in design.

Be fair: blame the workman, not his tools

The apparent weaknesses of PowerPoint are about its misuse rather than anything being intrinsically wrong with the tool itself. It's like blaming the ballpoint pen for producing boring documents. You really can't blame PowerPoint for the bad thinking of those who jump in to use it.

PowerPoint is easy to use, but very hard to use well. It's like dancing – any fool can jive, but to see the full potential, watch a professional do it. PowerPoint is like 'painting by numbers' – it gives the illusion of craftsmanship but in fact it just gets you on the road to painting. This is about allowing anyone and everyone to have a go. Anyway, for most people PowerPoint is the only useful and usable show in town so far as presentations go.

PowerPoint has improved working lives

In the so-called 'good old days' we used slides of art work that cost £20 each and took experts two days to prepare. Or we had overhead transparencies (which are still a fine tool for small groups – you can even write on them).

When we moved to computer-generated graphics, the first projectors took hours to set up – three guns, each of which needed to be put in focus – and were very sensitive, one knock and you were done for. They cost £25,000, about the same as a concert grand piano. Now a superior digital product with a single lens as opposed to three, with auto-focus costs about £500, the price of a reasonable electric guitar.

Click on PowerPoint and there they are – a set of thirty templates. You choose one – there are only three or four that I find useful – you type in your presentation content and in about half an hour you have a half-decent presentation. However, this is only a draft. The dish is still raw.

You then put your slides into notes page format and work on simplifying the slide, above what is now suspiciously beginning to look just like your script. As with sauces, you reduce and you reduce. You are an intelligent human being and this is just the beginning of a long, iterative process.

Those who don't like it describe such presentations as 'death by PowerPoint'. However, from a presenter's perspective it's 'life by PowerPoint' because the relatively PC illiterate among us can work, refine and improve all through the night without backup. We have been liberated.

☒ brilliant do's and don'ts

Assume you are busy, busy, busy and have to get this presentation cracked quickly.

- Don't get obsessed with the pictorial side of things or elaboration – focus on the story and the overview.

- Do set up your template by starting with the Slide Master so that your style – font, bullet points, indents and so on – is consistent. Make sure it looks how you want it to look to start with.

- Do write a contents page – this gives you a format, and a series of signposts in the right order. This will vary from situation to situation but it helps the audience if they know that you know where you are going.

- Always have a heading on your slide that says 'Strategy', 'Objectives', 'Challenges' or whatever but never more than five or six words – never. And always in lower case – it's easier to read.

- Don't use more than five bullets or thirty words a slide, except for handouts.

- Don't forget to leave gaps for pictures and diagrams, which may come later.

- Don't worry: you will always overwrite to start with so regard this as your handout.

- Now fill in the gaps. Keep it all cryptic with your sort of words, avoid jargon and use simple visuals.

- Now focus on refining and reducing your presentation – it is your musical accompaniment and it's there to make you look good and your meaning clear. It's there to help you tell your story memorably.

- Don't rely on your own judgement: if you have time, pass it to an expert to tidy it all up, and at least take out the ugly bits – better still, ask for a professional touch.

Let's get more technical

Here is a list of things you need to do to stop you making stupid mistakes when making your own slides.

- Do not use subheads and sub-bullets.

- Do not have complex charts – five simple ones rather than one complex one is preferable.

- Do not muck around with fonts and colour schemes – choose a simple scheme and stick to it.

- Ariel and Times Roman are pretty well foolproof – fonts such as Tahoma may not be. If you insist on unusual fonts your lovely presentation may go awry with strange line breaks and with half the text lost.

- Avoid animations, transitions and sound effects unless you have expert backup.

- Do not type your script on screen and then read it out – have pity on the poor audience.

- Do not include elements that may not work on other computers – taking risks with technology is like accelerating on black ice, a recipe for ignominy.

- Do not assume that everyone has an up-to-date PC like you.

- Having said that, do buy an up-to-date laptop, which you will henceforth call the 'audiovisual backup device'. Do not call it a computer – IT departments get funny about stuff in their territory. AV devices are usually someone else's problem but backup devices are fine, provided they don't impinge on the IT budget.

- Recognise that there is a difference between producing slides for projection in a big room and handouts for takeaway. The two are not the same, but many people assume they are.

Things to do to your PC

- Modify your toolbar so that it is easier to work with – half the stuff there you don't need.

- Use the Slide Master, which you'll find under Master View – it enables you to store information about font, positioning for text and objects, bullet styles, background design and colour schemes to be applied to all your slides, including any you may add later. It also allows you to apply retrospective global changes – such as changing font or colour – to all your slides.

- Under Tools/Options/Save you'll find 'Allow fast saves' – turn it off because it inflates the size of the file, as well as making it more prone to corruption.

- Use PowerPoint help groups (for example, http://office.microsoft.com) for tips and short cuts.

- Find useful short cuts and keep a list of them – for example Shift F3 turns everything into capital letters, Ctrl B or I or U formats a highlighted section as bold, italic or underlined respectively.

- Check your presentation prints in grayscale.

- Watch news programmes to see how the experts use and develop graphics – study weather presentations on BBC and ITV for example.

- Most important of all, if you want to be competent with PowerPoint, practise, practise, practise.

- Use the following websites to get advice, help and ideas:
  - www.showcase-online.co.uk
  - www.rdpslides.com/pptfaq

Having spent a significant part of my life in advertising, I do not believe it's worth bringing in professionals unless you brief them properly. So if you are going to work well, with or without them, you need to apply the following rules.

☀ brilliant tips

- Practise PowerPoint. How can you expect to be any good unless you practise? Those with real talent start with two distinctive things, an eye for design and a job – which means they do little else other than slides morning, noon and night.

- Exercise self-discipline. I mentioned earlier the 'corporate porridge' imposed by corporate design templates. Well, unless you are the boss, stick to the rules and work within them. There are no prizes for being radical when radical is illegal.

- Work with experts. Learn techniques by working with PowerPoint experts. At very little cost, they will show you short cuts and effects you haven't understood before.

- Study design. Look at the BBC for instance – its journalists and designers don't use PowerPoint but they are usually good at design. So is the *FT*. So is the *Sun* – study how they make their audience focus. We are, as a bunch of business people, hopeless at design. Become a 'design junkie' – it's one of the skills for which the UK has a strong reputation.

- Use notes pages. These help you to get that critical point of distinguishing between what you think *you* need to say and what the audience needs to see.

- Fire the bullets. Try to do a presentation free of bullet points and see what happens – you might liberate yourself from the 'bam-bam-bam' effect they tend to have.

- Find out what you can't do. If there is any really legitimate criticism of PowerPoint it's that it masks incompetence, not just from the audience but also from the presenter. You need to discover what you can and can't do if you are going to get better at it.

- Focus on the 'big one' to start with. This is the Jack Welch thing, which says you need a killer strategic slide – one that clarifies your message in a devastatingly clear way. Learning to use PowerPoint can help you to break your thoughts into logic-sized lumps. Thinking more positively about visuals in presentations can take you from average to excellent, or apprentice to brilliant, really quickly.

- Never confuse handouts with screen works. Yet everybody does. We live in a laptop-sized world and when it comes to a larger audience we sometimes can't understand why what looked great in the office at 11.30pm on your PC looks dull in the Queen Elizabeth Hall the next day. Big is not beautiful – it's merely *bigger*. And the really embarrassing thing about bigger is that it magnifies amateurism. What we produce for handouts and what we show on screen are not the same.

- Never use the word 'deck'. This is the word made famous in the 1970s when IBM was more famous for its presentations than commercial success. Why does it worry me? It sounds big and heavy – as though you could stand on it. It also sounds violent – 'I'll deck you'. What it doesn't sound like is fun.

You have only one chance

There is only one 'first night' when you do a presentation. You can't come back the next day having ironed out the wrinkles. This is your Terminal Five moment. You can change anything *now* – but you can change nothing afterwards (apart perhaps from your job). So practise now, as though your life depended on it. PowerPoint can liberate and enable you to visualise how to make a presentation work brilliantly.

But don't be an idiot by being a DIY bodger. You can do a small-scale presentation off your own bat but, however much you play with it, don't try doing a bigger performance without design professionals. If you do, you'll regret it. After all, you are the script writer and performer. Get the professionals to do set design, effects and stage management – under your direction, of course.

You thought technical stuff was easy?

So you have a plan, you have a story and you even have some pretty good slides. What can go wrong?

- The venue is terrible with pillars that get in the way. You did check the room yourself? Ah, you left that to an assistant. Hmmm!
- It's got a terrible acoustics – errible coustic . . . oost . . . ic . . . You did at least check this didn't you? You didn't! That was like buying a suit without checking the size and without trying it on first. Lunatic!
- The projectors are underpowered so your subtle coloured slides look washed out – a bit like you'll do by the time you've finished your show.
- You decided to present using a laptop screen to twenty people. Huge error – tiny screen and an irritated audience.
- Headline fonts should be 44 point or thereabouts and text should not go below 20 point. Hard-to-read charts are the cardinal sin. Bravely you ignore this and watch in dismay as all these myopic sixty-year-olds walk into the room. Pity but they won't be able to read the slides at all. Are you in trouble!

Anyway, you're ready to roll – here are some reminders.

Summary

- Don't read the slides.
- Have cryptic notes on your notes page, which you use as your script guide.

- Writing good scripts is a *very, very* different art to writing an article, an e-mail or a book.
- Your script is there for you and no one else – so have it in huge print and short sentences.
- Avoid big slabs of text – you'll lose your place.
- The best presenters go through a five-stage process:
  - think;
  - notes;
  - script;
  - cryptic script;
  - notes.
- Always write your own scripts because reading other people's scripts is lazy and will consign you forever to being a boring novice.
- Do not allow yourself to overrun – this is a crime equivalent to burglary because you are stealing the audience's time.
- Pauses are good . . . long pauses can have a dramatic effect. Important though the audience is, make it clear that you are in charge of this pause and that you haven't simply dried in blind terror. One speaker employed the dramatic pause too liberally and someone in the audience stood up and asked 'Are you all right?'

But most important of all are these three things:

- **Plan** so that you really know what you are trying to do.
- **Rehearse** so you leave nothing to chance. This does not mean going through your presentation so many times that you get bored with it. It means knowing it well enough to know what comes next and to know where the high spots come.
- **Spend twice as long** as you are used to on preparing presentations and do as many as you can. It is only with

practice that you'll improve. Have you, for instance, ever heard of an accomplished linguist who spoke French, or whatever, only once a year? The harsh truth in life is that you have to work hard. As the golfer Gary Player said: 'You know, the more I practise the luckier I get.'

However, it also makes great sense to check regularly what you are doing right and not-so-right as a presenter. Do it with a professional, someone who is constantly exposed to different presenters. This will be refreshing and expose the faults that in isolation may not be a big problem but which in combination may be holding you back.

The final, critical point – enjoy yourself! No, that's not a joke. But how, you ask, how can you enjoy standing up there with shaking legs and the strong feeling that you now know what the onset of a heart attack feels like? By getting used to being good – that's how. And when you've done a brilliant presentation, just the once, the euphoria will make you feel amazing and you'll find that you won't be able to wait for your next outing.

brilliant tip

Work with a professional, someone who is constantly exposed to different presenters

CHAPTER 10

The book as a presentation

W hat follows is this book in PowerPoint. It shows how the software is relatively easy to master. It also shows how good design can lift an OK presentation to something nearer music.

Following my own advice ... almost

I followed my own advice in reducing some of the advice in this book into a fifteen-minute PowerPoint presentation – but I did it much too fast. There is a torrent of bullet points – a long stretch of sleeping policemen to destroy the axle of comprehension. And I have the design talent of a five-year-old.

Discovering what really happens

Creating a *basic* presentation is a breeze – not brilliant but competent. PowerPoint, much derided by many, allows you to simplify your thoughts in a helpful way. What is here is a focus on *key thoughts* but the visual material is dull. At this stage this is just a good brief. Raw meat. Not a meal. Not yet.

Brilliant presenting requires a balance of a bunch of elements, but most of the time presenters are trying to avoid one or more of the disasters on the next page.

Impediments to brilliance

Potential disasters include:

● dying on stage;

● drying on stage;

● slides that are uncorrected or unreadable or plain wrong;

● technical breakdowns – no mike, mike muffle or boom; the laptop crashes;

● an electrical blackout;

● a different audience to the one anticipated – 'no one said Bill Gates was coming!';

● a *sudden* realisation that this is not an appropriate presentation for the audience.

Most of us are cautious when exposing ourselves to potential ridicule – rightly so. But being merely competent and having the chance to excel are not simple alternatives. Avoiding disasters and being brilliant are not bedfellows – one is defensive, the other aggressive.

Nearly all the potential disasters mentioned above are under your control, assuming you've got your nerves sorted out. Assume that you've done your homework – so you know about the coming of Mr Gates. He's just a normal bloke with lots on his mind and a short attention span, but this is *your* show and the *audience's*, not his. Carry on and sock it to them, and if he is socked too then great.

The presentation that follows isn't inappropriate because it is descriptive and apolitical. The only time you'll encounter the inappropriate issue is in the over-bold use of risky humour, indiscretion and poor understanding of what is needed (read Chapter 4 again).

How to do brilliant presentations

The three presentations that follow are based on what this book is trying to achieve, starting with the basic Version A. Version B shows what effect a little effort can have and Version C shows what a craftsman can do.

Version A

These are just notes at this stage – the shape of a story, a plot-line if you like. They might do for a handout. But the bones are there.

Planning is the key

Decide:-
  - WHY are you doing it
  - To WHOM are you doing it
  - WHAT is your story
  - HOW are you going to bring it alive
  - WHERE is it happening
  - HOW MUCH can you spend

Context

- What's going on in the world
- What's going on in the company
- What's going on with the brand
- What's going on with you
- What's going on with your audience

What's the story

- Key message

- The 'rule of three'

- Big start

- Bigger finish

- Checklist:

  - Simple
  - Less is more
  - Seize attention
  - Be memorable
  - Demand action

Getting in the colour

- Stories need descriptions
- Stories need anecdotes
- Stories need personal touches
- Stories need to be contemporary
- Stories need 'quotes'

Performing with power

- Control your nerves
  - breathe better
  - out of body confidence
- Be a bigger you
- Use your voice
- ACT – this is theatre
- Listen to the audience

  'Isn't it easier to act old boy?' (Sir Laurence Olivier)

Good slides will help

- Less is more
- But use more slides if this simplifies
- Slides are accelerators not brakes
- Don't look like everyone else
- Use your first draft as notes
- Get help to improve

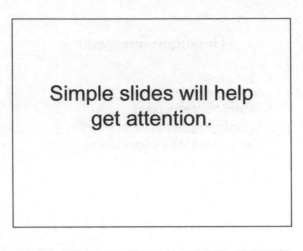

Simple slides will help get attention.

Practice makes perfect

- **Plan**
  - what you say
  - the story line
  - the surprises
  - the context
  - the performance

- **Performance**
  - use pros to help
  - do run-throughs
  - simplify
  - rehearse
  - rehearse
  - get backup staff on your side

The stuff that gets forgotten

Before

- Agendas are like menus
- Things on seats set expectation
- Know your audience

After

- This is networking time
- E-mail presentation
- Keep their cards
- Answer their questions

How good are you?

1. Novice
2. Apprentice
3. Craftsman
4. Star
5. Brilliant

Getting better

Just three things:

1. Be honest about where you are now
2. Work on your material so you have a strong story
3. Practise like crazy

Summary

- Presentations can make you richer
- Plan how to get better
- Plan your next one better
- Spend more time on it
- Focus on: Context, Story, Colour, Slides, Performance, Before/After
- Work. Work. Work
- Get pros to help you

Version B

This shows the effect of a tidy-up but not much more than that – it's a haircut not a makeover. An editor let loose on too many words.

Simplicity is a friend to comprehension. As you simplify slides, making them more straightforward and with fewer bullet points, you should (I hope) see that your audience has a better chance of following you and the slide dancing together – as opposed to you doing a Foxtrot and the slide doing the Gay Gordons.

This process takes time, just like cooking a sauce and reducing it to the perfect taste and consistency. This presentation is bubbling now but it still isn't cooked yet.

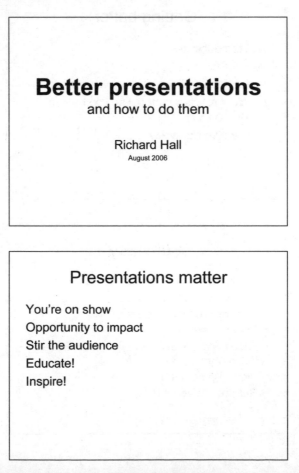

Planning is key

Decide:
- WHY you are doing it
- WHO you are doing it to
- WHAT your story is
- HOW you will bring it alive
- WHERE it is happening
- HOW MUCH you can spend

Context

What's going on:
- in the world
- in the company
- with the brand
- with you
- with your audience

What's the story

- One big idea
- The 'rule of three'
- Big start
- Bigger finish

Checklist:
- Simple
- Less is more
- Seize attention
- Be memorable
- Demand action

Getting in the colour

Stories need:
- descriptions
- anecdotes
- personal touches
- relevance
- 'quotes'

Be a bigger you

Performing with power

- Use your nerves / breathe better
- Out of body confidence
- Use your voice
- Act – this is theatre
- Listen to the audience

Good slides help

- Less is more
- Break down complexity
- Slides are accelerators not brakes
- Be different
- Don't put your script on the slide
- Get the right support

Simple slides grab attention

Practice makes perfect

Plan
- What you say
- The story line
- The surprises
- The context
- The performance

Performance
- Use professionals to help
- Do run-throughs
- Simplify
- Rehearse
- Rehearse
- Get backup staff on side

The stuff that gets forgotten

Before

- Agendas are like menus
- Things on seats set expectations
- Know your audience

After

- This is networking time
- E-mail presentation
- Keep their cards
- Answer their questions

How good are you?

1 Novice
2 Apprentice
3 Craftsman
4 Star
5 Brilliant

Getting better

1 Be honest about where you are now

2 Work on your material so you have a strong story

3 Practise like crazy

Summary

- Presentations can make you richer
- Plan how to get better
- Plan your next one better
- Spend more time on it
- Focus on: context, story, colour, slides, performance, before/after
- Work – Work – Work
- Get professionals to help you

Version C

Enter the designer. The use of colour (use your imagination or check on my website, www.richardhall.biz) makes a big difference. Images, shape, drama – all these make a presentation better to look at and more fun to do.

Why the lemon? Being ironic and smart I could say 'to give it zest' because this is what it does. But I could also say 'to give it vitamin C' where 'C' stands for communication. It sets the literal message off in an appealing way.

Lemons, like presentations, are enigmatic things – they look like fruit and they smell fruity, but they are quite tart. They also give the presentation dimension and dynamic continuity. The lemon changes – it is not a logo – it goes through various recognisable conformations. It's an active not a passive lemon.

Yet this is only the start of the design process that shows how to begin improving the speed and impact of communication.

Better presentations
and how to do them

Richard Hall
August 2006

Presentations matter

You're on show!

Opportunity to impact!

Stir the audience!

Educate!

Inspire!

Planning is key

Decide

WHY you are doing it
WHO you are doing it to
WHAT your story is
HOW you will bring it alive
WHERE it is happening
HOW MUCH you can spend

Context

What's going on:
In the world
In the company
With the brand
With you
With your audience

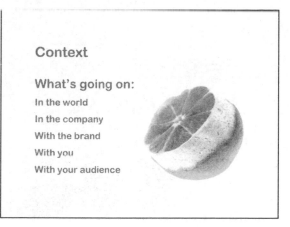

What's the story

1 big idea	**Checklist:**
The "rule of three"	Simple
Big start	Less is more
Bigger finish	Seize attention
	Be memorable
	Demand action

Getting in the colour

Stories need:
Descriptions
Anecdotes
Personal touches
Relevance
"Quotes"

Be a
bigger

Performing with power

Use your nerves / breathe better
Out of body confidence
Use your voice
Act – this is theatre
Listen to the audience

Good slides help

Less is more
Break down complexity
Slides are accelerators not brakes
Be different
Don't put your script on the slide
Get the right support

Simple
slides
grab
attention!

Practice makes perfect

Plan	Performance
What you say	Use pros to help
The story line	Do run-throughs
The surprises	Simplify
The context	Rehearse
The performance	Rehearse
	Get back-up-staff on side

The stuff that gets forgotten

Before	After
Agendas are like menus	This is networking time
Things on seats set expectations	E-mail presentation
Know your audience	Keep their cards
	Answer their questions

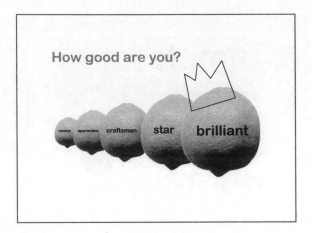

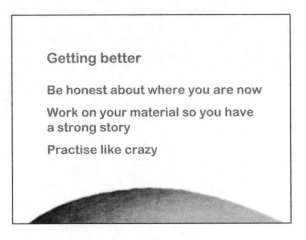

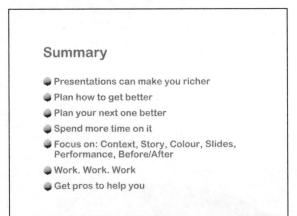

CHAPTER 11

Really understanding your audience

You have all the talent in the world, have practised like crazy with a tight, solid story that is beautifully illustrated, and you understand the context in which you are appearing – and yet things can still go wrong.

You have to do more – you have to *really* understand your audience.

Brilliance wrecked by not listening

I recently heard the story about a well-known performer at conferences – known as a 'motivational speaker'. These are often terrifying people who have manic staring eyes and who speak very quickly using a lot of acronyms – 'TEAM – together everyone achieves more'. He arrived late owing to terrible traffic caused by an accident on the A1. Even Mr Motivational Cool was breathing a bit heavily as he rushed into the conference centre for the annual Spartemex conference. His contact from the company rushed up to him, 'Thank God you're here – we were so worried – you're on pretty well right away and they really need cheering up a bit – everyone's very down because . . .'. 'No time . . . sorry. I'm bursting for a pee and I need just two minutes alone to get my head together. See you by the stage.'

Two minutes later he sprang on stage giving big eye contact and bellowing 'Hello Spartemex – and how are we today?' Silence.

Virtually everyone was looking down. 'Come on boys and girls get it together because you are a great team and you know what TEAM means – T . . . E . . . A . . . M – together everyone achieves more.' A girl in the front row stood up looked at him (at last a reaction) burst into tears and rushed off down the aisle howling. After half an hour he staggered off stage having tried everything and got no reaction apart from people shaking their heads and walking out.

He spotted his Spartemex contact. 'What was all that about? That is the only disaster I've ever had and the worst audience I've ever come across.' His contact shook her head sadly. 'You were in such a state when you arrived that you didn't give me a chance to explain, and then you just pushed past me to get on stage. Our deputy chairman collapsed on stage in the middle of his speech of welcome and died. We all loved him. Everyone's feeling bereft.'

Mr Motivation had wondered about the ambulance that nearly drove him off the road as he made his hurried approach to the building.

Lessons in how to understand audiences

● Always make sure that you are clearly and fully briefed, especially on any areas of sensitivity. The marketing director is Irish, no Irish jokes; the new chief is a mathematician, no jokes at all; the deputy chairman has just died on stage, don't be jolly.

brilliant tip

Make sure that the speaker is always clearly and fully briefed, especially on any areas of sensitivity

- However hyped up you are, whatever process you use to get your adrenalin going, do not turn off your brain. Listen, look around, understand.

- Know your audience. Who are they? What do they know? What do they want? Why are they here? What do they know about you?

- When in doubt don't dig yourself into a hole. It's never stupid to get among the audience and see how they feel. And, by the way, never overestimate your ability to change the mood of a meeting.

- Not all, or indeed many, audiences are homogeneous. Understand all the undercurrents. Do not present radical material to dyed-in-the-wool conservatives and expect applause. Don't invest your money on a potentially losing hand when you don't even understand the game you are playing. Get, or try to get, the audience on your side.

- Don't be boring. Get to the nub of what will 'sell'.

- Don't drink or carouse too soon before a presentation because it slows the brain.

- If you are presenting as a team then get it together. Never let one player go off dribbling the ball alone. Applause does not mean a good review. Pleasing people with your presentation is not the same as winning with it. You are there to win, not entertain.

- Listen to where your audience is and what they want. Indulge them, hit the hot buttons. And if you press a button and nothing happens, move on.

brilliant example

A presentation to NBC Super Channel

No one had heard of it in the UK at the time. It now seems to be a cable channel. It's frankly rather confusing. Back in the mid 1990s I discovered one hotel – the Hyde Park as I recall – that was testing it out.

Being an energetic spirit I booked in, ate room service food, drank beer and watched the channel from 7pm till 2am. Now, I never watch much TV except when I have flu so this was a strange experience. I watched people talking about their health – their legs, bowel movements and breathlessness – a session on share prices, some baseball, a chat show with Jay Leno and, as I got sleepier, I seem to recall some soft porn.

In our straightforward presentation, in which boxes were being ticked or not, I had a slot in which to review the product and as time passed it seemed that I was probably the only person in the room (including those from NBC) who had an intimate and extensive experience of the product.

When I came to talk about it I must have taken leave of my senses. I extemporised and exaggerated about Jay Leno, about vitamin pills, about the business correspondent's cleavage ('the Dow's well down this evening ...'). I even managed to make baseball sound funny.

The guys and girls from NBC were in hysterics. My own team was laughing but in a slightly bemused 'follow that' sort of way. When it came to it, my contribution was funny but unfocused. Judge a presentation not by the applause but by the reviews – ours were not good and we did not win the business. Never let the performance devour the plot. Upstaging? Eat your heart out Brad Pitt. The NBC team left thanking me, ignoring the rest of the boring team (yes, they were very boring) and drying their eyes.

brilliant tip

Not only know your audience but also feel their feelings, needs and hopes

Overall, you should not only know your audience but also feel their feelings, needs and hopes. You should respond to the vibes you get – and if you don't feel any, provoke some. You need to work with the minds of people in the audience and develop what is going on in there.

I have often been asked to speak at weddings, funerals, birthdays and other events. The brilliant thing about these is that the audiences are:

- full of politics – families always have undercurrents;
- replete with landmines – don't make any German, Irish, mother-in-law or whatever jokes (as if I would);
- focused on the event in question;
- friendly – willing you to succeed;
- diverse in age and sensitivity;
- waiting to be entertained;
- or undergo a catharsis.

I've had more satisfaction and learned more about the pure art of presentation doing these than anything else. Focusing on the subject and making sure that you romance, dramatise and make the subject look good is everything. Being upbeat and optimistic always works – even at funerals. Not 'This is a catastrophic tragedy' so much as 'She died too young – of course – but look at all the great stuff she did while she was alive – and boy, was she alive.'

But most of all these occasions are about gauging the mood of, listening to, responding to and trying to achieve a real connection with the audience. They are also nerve-racking. 'I thought that strategic presentation was wrong – can we discuss the key elements?' is not what you ever want to hear, but the following is far worse: 'The family and I are very upset. I'm sorry but he was nothing like the man you described.' By getting the tone wrong I have seen people create havoc at both funerals and weddings.

Summary

The audience is always right, so it's your job to understand them not theirs to understand you. You are the magician so make magic. Given the opportunity to do any speeches, celebratory or valedictory or quite simply any presentations to a real audience, do them. They are a wonderful experience and you only discover the core truths of presenting when you do it live, core truths such as these:

- knowing your audience;
- knowing your subject;
- writing a great, positive, good natured essay;
- simplifying it;
- practising and practising;
- using splashes of colour;
- aiming to entertain;
- listening and responding to your audience;
- relaxing with them and finding they love you;
- acting it so you achieve maximum effect.

CHAPTER 12

From ordinary to brilliant

y now you'll have made a few discoveries about yourself and about some of the techniques you need to be brilliant. My guess is that you'll be discovering that you are doing better than you'd ever thought and that, with just a bit more effort, you could be even better. Don't worry because you are in good company.

Until now presentation has not been in pole position for you but now it's time for a change. Because becoming a brilliant presenter is the most important, career-defining thing you can do. This being so, do it.

A change and a commitment

I want you to make me a promise – on your next presentation I want you to triple the amount of time you spend on it. Before you get too far into it, I want you to score yourself on each of the following on a scale 0–5, where 5 represents 'brilliant' and 0 equals 'appalling':

- context;
- story;
- colour;
- illustration;
- performance.

Scoring anything over 18 will mean you are approaching the 'brilliance zone'.

You will discover that you will achieve an instant improvement just by focusing on this framework. But the real keys now lie with the content. If you know that you have a compelling story you will feel more confident and more inclined to go that extra mile. So I want you to spend a long time (through the night if needs be) on the content – the story and the colours you want to introduce.

The good news is you'll be astounded by the level of improvement you achieve. The bad news is you'll be very tired and if you aren't tired you aren't working hard enough at it.

Getting the story right will drive everything else

This is not going to be easy because you are probably straying into unfamiliar territory, where the idea of building a brilliantly compelling story is alien to the way you work. What I'm asking for is something that is:

- descriptive and vivid;
- informative;
- attention-grabbing.

And this requires a lot of hard work.

Take a piece of paper and start making notes – anything that comes into your brain. Circle words that seem as though they might make themes – growth, competitive pressure, innovation, change, consumer insight, global competition, customer loyalty and so on, you know, the kind of words around which others cluster.

It is here that brilliance has to kick in, the brilliance of making connections.

How do brilliant presenters do it?

They generally apply one of four approaches that you will recognise when you see them at work. They may also work for you.

- The power of intelligence. This is the application of considered thinking. People like academics, senior civil servants or experts in their field use this to great effect.

- The presenter as commentator. This is where irony is used or where the speaker sees things from several points of view and comments on the viewpoints. This is a common source of deadpan humour.

- 'I am very clever but I don't take myself too seriously.' There is nothing better than seeing the big boss acting like a human being, or an expert speaking to non-experts at their level without being patronising. Not being too serious is a great way of getting very serious points across.

- Deep knowledge lets you be very simple and very certain. Simon Walker, chief executive of the British Private Equity and Venture Capital Association, talks of people who casually allude to something whilst appearing to have pocketfuls of knowledge about it should they choose to reveal it. It's always great to hear an expert talk about their stuff, whether a sportsman or Bill Clinton. In your case talk about what you really know and it will have the same effect.

brilliant tips to take you into the brilliant zone

- Safety last. When doing a presentation, our instincts are to retreat into mediocrity. A 'brave presentation' has the same sound to it as the immortal 'that is a courageous decision minister' in the BBC series *Yes Minister* (decoded this means it is a rash and possibly career-damaging decision). Yet it is impossible to be a brilliant presenter if you only ever play safe.

Rupert Howell, managing director of the commercial arm of ITV, was known to sing at the start of a presentation when he was in advertising. Bartholomew Sayle, who ran the Breakthrough Group, did the same to prove how far out on a limb he'd be prepared to put himself. I did it in a wedding speech recently. That's taking risks – and if you heard my voice you'd realise this is very high risk indeed. Who knows what Sebastian Coe did at the presentation of the London Olympics bid but we can be sure it wasn't ordinary.

My brother-in-law used to say 'boldness be my friend' before playing a slightly risky shot in golf – and, surprisingly, it often is.

- Steal brilliant ideas. It was Picasso who said 'amateurs borrow, professionals steal' and if you want to be brilliant you must, above all, be professional. The other line I like is that if you borrow one thought it's called stealing, but if you borrow lots it's called research. So get your swag bag out and get stealing.

For a start, watch the best stand-up comedians and see how they work. Watch Jack Dee and see how he became 'king of laid back'. This happened because he failed as an enthusiastic comic. In the last few performances before finally jacking it in, he stopped really trying and adopted the characteristic Jack 'sod-it' Dee mode. The audience response was ecstatic, and the rest is history. Watch my namesake Rich Hall for controlled anger and for going off on an amazing rant about accountants or whatever seizes his mind that night. Watch Jo Brand to see the mistress of measured exposition and irony. Watch Rowan Atkinson to see submerged mania threatening you and a focused delivery where every word is like a sharp knife. On a more serious note (but not much more serious) watch Andrew Neill on the BBC's *This Week* to see a presentational tour de force being exploited by someone who uses every trick available.

Take every chance you can to see professionals at work then nick their best stuff, techniques and attitudes that seem to work for you – be shameless.

● Less is more. As a simple rule, this alone will drive you to brilliance most compellingly. It was well recognised, not least by Mark Twain, that it is harder to write good short pieces than good long pieces. Stream of consciousness is easy but sonnets or haiku are harder to write than ballads.

Reducing your presentation to its perfect state takes effort and time. Too many presentations are, as it were, undercooked – the sauce is thin and runny, the ingredients haven't blended together. When you are pulling your presentation together have a blue pencil beside you which is your 'brilliance editor'. I heard recently yet another great reason for using cryptic charts from Ian Parker, strategy head of one of the key divisions at Zurich Financial Services: 'Do not trap yourself beneath a welter of words on a slide. How embarrassing to have "Growth is continuing to grow fast" when you have a sudden embarrassing sales hiccough. The single word "growth" allows you flexibility.' He's right. I suppose you could manage to say 'Growth has been great but can it continue? Look at last month when we had poor sales. Yet the underlying story is still good if we can get our sales momentum back. It also serves to show that you can take nothing for granted and that you can never take your eye off the ball.' This, of course, is what modern management must have – the flexibility to respond to events as they occur.

Too many people inadvertently treat their presentations as suicide notes. Stories of the day before yesterday and worse ... their ill-digested, uncooked ramblings on screen may help them keep on track but pity the poor audience. The next time you review a presentation that you are going to give make sure you ask: 'How can I reduce the stuff in here? How can I take words

out of the slides? How can I achieve clear focus on the issues?'
Ensuring you are cryptic and that you aim for less is great
advice because, as we know, less is more.

- Being very brilliant means being 'very something ...' The
  danger of being too reserved lies in simple human nature – in
  wanting to disappear into the crowd. As our nerves get worse
  we want to hide under the blanket, sucking our thumb. But we
  need to be very brave to be outstanding. Here are some
  options:

  - Be very learned: this works brilliantly if you are very learned
    and if you have the material to carry it off.

  - Be very funny: this is all about risk and reward. Clint
    Eastwood as Dirty Harry said 'Do you feel lucky punk? Well
    do you?' I feel much the same about humour in business. It
    is best avoided unless you are very sure of yourself and even
    then ...

  - Be very theatrical: this can work brilliantly depending on the
    personality of the presenter and the nature of the audience.

  - Be very confident: this will always work provided 'confident'
    doesn't become 'cocky'. Confident presenters calm an
    audience's fears and hostility; very confident presenters
    inspire them.

  - Be very smart: it is brilliant to be presented to by someone
    who convinces you that they really understand what's going
    on in a consumer's mind. George Davis, creator of the Per
    Una fashion range for Marks and Spencer, was convincing in
    his claim that he really, really understood women and what
    they wanted. He always sounded smart and on the ball.

  - Be very cross: I don't recommend this unless you are Tom
    Peters who rants and raves and gets paid a fortune for doing it.

- Be very enthusiastic: far too many managers in business seem worn down by their bosses or by the rigours of the job to the point that they seem unenthusiastic, weary and bored. Enthusiasm in presentations can lift you into the 'brilliance zone' faster than anything else I can think of.

- Brilliance lies in pubs and shops, not at desks. This is a serious point. People working with other people will, on balance, be more likely to produce brilliant stuff than people flying solo. Brilliance is found outside yourself, not inside. What you do is provide the electricity that links the elements together. Tom Peters said 'No one ever wasted money travelling' and he's right, insofar as the brutal reality of getting out from behind your desk and seeing new things can make you do and think more brilliantly. Heathrow will inspire you. It doesn't? It doesn't? Smack! Heathrow *will* inspire you – a vast city of transit and shops. Even and perhaps especially Terminal Five. Yes, truly, all human life is there. It's a market researcher's delight. Spend time listening, looking, tasting, touching and smelling. You'll learn more about human nature in the perfumerie in Selfridges, Harvey Nichols or Harrods than you ever will in an office. You'll learn more having a good lunch with an engaging friend than you will reading *The Times*, which should take only 20 minutes to do anyway; hopefully lunch will take longer. Brilliance comes from listening, absorbing and then recreating. Brilliance doesn't exist in an intellectual monastery or nunnery.

- 'Yes you can ...' Brilliance will only come from pushing yourself and giving yourself terrifying challenges. A challenge which evokes 'I really honestly couldn't do that, it's just beyond me – honestly', but which when met lifts you to new heights. One of the people I coached seemed unlikely ever to be a competent presenter. I'd now describe them as close to brilliant. The lesson to be learned is that you will find that you achieve brilliance quicker by working with coaches.

● Trust in yourself. As I was lining up to play a tee shot over a lake, someone said to me 'Trust in your swing'. Only years after that inevitable splash from a topped drive did I really work out quite what lay behind this. If you don't believe in the equipment and talent you have then you are in a very bad place. Be the first to praise yourself – be the first to say how great the good bits were and be confident enough to criticise the poorer bits.

There is one piece of advice I want you to copy and put in your pocket if your quest to be a brilliant presenter is genuine:

You are a brilliant presenter. Be yourself. Be active. Be fun. Every presentation you do is a 'crunch'. So just do it freshly, enthusiastically and with rigour. You can be a brilliant presenter. But start by feeling brilliant.

● Write yourself a letter. This is an extension of what appears above and a tool with quite amazing impact. Brilliance can only happen in an environment where praise is bestowed. Apart from painters like Cezanne who had a rotten time in their life, most great artists and, by definition, most great performers, require praise to deliver the goods. So help yourself. Write that letter – 'Dear Richard, I want you to know you were great yesterday – really inspiring and funny but, more to the point totally focused … it was great to be there … you were brilliant.' Self-indulgent? Ridiculous? Unnecessary? No – not if it achieves the key aim of making you improve and become, hopefully, brilliant.

● Be in a good mood. It's really hard being brilliant when you are grumpy. One of the reasons that so many politicians become less effective as they spend more time in office is that they get worn down by intransigent issues. They become fed up, irritable and frustrated and their one-time brilliance is blunted. So the next time you start to prepare a presentation, and especially as you actually perform, think hard about how happy you are and how glad you are to be doing it especially to this particular audience whom you particularly like.

- Be incurably curious. The stuff of all brilliant presentations is the unusual, the surprising and the novel. It's also true that people who have a big appetite for life and an unquenchable interest in it are generally the most entertaining company. Great presenters describe things vividly with the excitement of someone seeing something for the first time. They have a childlike sense of curiosity and an appetite for discovery, so try to be like them. The best example I have of this was at the Hay-on-Wye book festival. Germaine Greer was running a master class on Blake's poem *The Sick Rose*. The poem is only eight lines long and she spent over an hour dissecting it. This was one of the best hours I've spent for a long time. This curvy and now mature Australian sat on a chair in the centre of the stage and talked fast and intensely. She demonstrated fierce curiosity. She really wanted to know what the poem meant. She interrogated it, rained questions down on it and was a restless source of 'don't get it, don't know, don't know yet'. She wrestled with the words and pulled each one to the ground where she pummelled the meaning out of it. It was completely absorbing and totally brilliant.

CHAPTER 13

Graduation to brilliance

elax. You've attained brilliance. People look at you in awe. They think you should become an actor. Those who don't know you think that if you are not an actor then you are someone important in the media. But you, poor thing, remain paranoid, frail and lacking in self-confidence. It doesn't get any easier does it? You work harder, you get better and you know more of the tricks to get you by at any presentation you have to do. But constantly pay attention because this is theatre and in theatre every performance is different. That's what makes it so much fun, as well as being a bit dangerous.

A scale of improvement

Let us suppose that you've done a lot of presenting and that you have become quite accomplished. When someone uses the 'P word' nowadays you don't feel a frisson of terror or hear the *Psycho* music. You just know it's 'presentation time' not 'shower curtain time' and that everything is all right.

You've stopped using the word 'presentation' though and just to help you and those around you to define the scale of an event you talk about presentations as:

- conversations;
- talks;

- gigs;
- shows.

Everyone knows that a 'show' involves the whole kit and will be full of appropriate effects and surprises – although the art of keeping surprises to a minimum is what characterises all the analysts' presentations anyone gets involved with.

Brilliant presenters, like you've become, are also pragmatists. Not every performance can be as brilliant as you'd wish, not every innings is a century, not every round of golf is a 65, not every meal is Michelin three star, not every day is cloudless. In the real world, and this is what makes live performance so utterly thrilling, there is variation in product. The story will be more, or less, convincing. The performer will be less, or more, on song.

brilliant tip

Not every performance can be as brilliant as you'd wish, not every innings can be a century

However, one thing will be absolutely constant and that will be your enthusiasm to improve. The better you get, the more self-critical you will become and the more time you will spend on trying to lift your game. And remember, you will seldom if ever be perfect. Perfection and brilliance are not the same thing. Brilliance is amazing; perfection is admirable but chilling.

brilliant tips that even brilliant presenters have to remember

- Controlling nerves. Mark Twain said: 'There are two types of speakers, those that are nervous and those that are liars.' Even the best get butterflies and sometimes they get a shock. Like a sudden urge to do a runner, or a new sensation such as trembling or the desire to go and have a pee. Tony Jeary has written a book *Inspire Any Audience* in which he confesses (he's called 'Mr Presentation' – I'm not joking – Mr Presentation!) 'I'm always nervous before a presentation; the day I'm not nervous is the day I quit presenting.'

I've discussed controlling nerves earlier. Having got to this stage of accomplishment it is unlikely that you're going to be scared speechless but you will get butterflies; and by the way the collective of butterflies is a 'rainbow of butterflies'. I rather like the thought of going on stage with a rainbow of butterflies coursing through one's veins. That sounds exciting but I also found another collective that brilliantly describes what it's like when you don't feel so good – 'a rabble of butterflies'. Those we can do without. Go for a rainbow not a rabble.

For all you brilliant presenters regard this as a management exercise. You must remain bodily and mentally self-aware, so those signals your body gives – 'I'm not feeling great today, I feel a bit sick; I've got a headache; I feel rather lethargic' – are dealt with and placed under control with a dictatorial self-rebuke: 'Feel like that later – not now.' In presenting, feeling in control of yourself is the key to delivering well. And I call this 'taming the butterflies'.

- Enthusiasm sells. So overflow with it. Occasionally you have to deliver bad news to people but the roots of motivation lie in inspiring them. And there's too little of that happening right now. I think all cynics should be put out of their misery to prevent anyone suffering their destructive gloom. Brilliant people can usually explain bad news well and offer the prospect of good news if certain courses of action are followed. Lady Thatcher used to say of Lord Young – then just plain David – 'Other people bring me problems; David brings me solutions.'

Brilliant people or communicators are seldom cockeyed optimists but they always, in my experience, exude the belief that there is a solution even if it will take effort to achieve it. Intriguingly, James Lovelock, author of *The Revenge of Gaia*, finds it possible to juxtapose the thoughts that 'as far as global warming is concerned the game is over' with 'but as far as individual countries are concerned, by focusing on solutions rather than global rhetoric, I am very optimistic' – particularly as far as Holland and the UK are concerned. Like it or not, audiences seldom respond to (or remember) presentational diatribes or whackings. However, they do often respond to good-natured stroking and visions of the future.

We remember speeches like Harold Wilson's first as Labour party leader when he talked about the thrill of technological advance and said: 'This party is a moral crusade or it is nothing.' They liked David Cameron when he spoke – no, presented – at the Conservative party conference and became the new leader because he spoke to their hopes for a new future and – good presentation trick – because he spoke without notes. This meant he really delivered his message from his inner being – it was about his beliefs (which he didn't need to write down) not a speech (which was a presentation). Clever of him and his advisors to spot the difference.

● A funny thing happened on the way to the presentation. Humour, like adrenalin, is dangerous stuff in presenting – too much and you can lose your audience for good. No one likes a second-rate comedian and the art of joke-telling to a few people, let alone a roomful, is highly specialised. Tommy Cooper had the ability, like Helge Fisher, the Pilates teacher, who advocates the need 'to be' silently on stage for quite a long time before you begin to think of 'talking'. Tommy would simply stand there, shrug and laugh and the whole of the Palladium would be in stitches. The only brilliant presenters I've seen who have a great feel for humour are Tony O'Reilly and Richard Eyres. The rest avoid the joke – they believe the risk is much higher than potential reward – but every brilliant presenter tells a colourful story with ironic asides. On balance, going for smiles and chuckles rather than belly laughs is the way forward. And remember how the audience feels – no one wants Mr Grumpy. Good nature and good humour are powerful tools.

● On the magic art of delegation. The mark of the most senior brilliant presenters is they will have a reliable team of professionals around them, certainly for all their gigs and shows. These will comprise a team to make the slides look great and work properly, a mentor to help ensure the material sounds good and that the story is communicating powerfully, people in charge of sound, lights, stage and so on, and a PA who has an even better memory than them. They will know all these people – they don't risk using untried hired guns – and these people know them. Hopefully, they also enjoy working with each other.

Most of us have less room for manoeuvre and smaller budgets at our disposal. You will – if you are smart – be doing a small amount of work with a professional communications expert and a slide producer to lift your game. DIY PowerPoint is very easy to spot and marks you out as a hands-on maverick. In 'conversations' and 'talks' that's fine – in bigger events it's frankly a little disappointing, as anyone who has done this will probably know to their cost.

● The voice is the key. Or, at any rate, it is key to performance. There are some really talented voice coaches around. I've worked with the brilliant Suzi Grant, the former Sky TV presenter and now a best-selling author on nutrition and ageing. Her technique can best be described as the energetic and friendly pummelling of a victim until, viewing themselves on video, they start to project, to deepen and to pace their delivery. What she does to brilliant presenters is to make them act with their voices, use them as instruments. Her own voice is deep, throaty and rich with laughter – imagine if you can Fenella Fielding crossed with Mariella Frostrup.

Although I haven't worked with them, I've heard good things about Angie Konrad of Voicewaves and Chris Hughes Prior of Speech-Works Plus. Chris asks people if they sound 'rushed, lightweight or strained'. To which I imagine them squeaking 'What me? Not at all – erm – no, no not lightweight, Ha! Ha!' She and a wide range of voice trainers across the world are transforming people's job prospects because they've been helped to sound convincing even though their performance in their jobs may not be immediately improving.

However brilliant you are and have been, don't neglect the presenter's number one tool – the voice. Every so often go for a check-up – that's if you're going to do a lot of presentations and are going to stay brilliant at doing them.

● What is your voice? Who are you? When James Wilde, the deposed chief of Rentokil, said in indignation in his dying days 'I am a CEO, not an actor' he was right in one sense. Actors, like slide makers, give their all to their craft and are focused professionals. No doubt Terence Stamp would have delivered James' speech with more conviction but he would almost certainly have been a worse executive. Yet you have to act. You may even have to lie or, at best, prevaricate. You may have to look relatively upbeat when you know your new wonder drug is doing poorly in tests. Honesty is not always the best policy. Timing how and when to break bad news calls for the skills of an actor.

So decide what you are comfortable about:

- How you sound: I've advocated voice training. You need it, whoever you are, but you need to be the designer of this voice and have a strong sense of how *you* want it to sound and develop.

- Who you are: or, how you are perceived. For example, Sir Michael Edwardes, one of the most admired businessmen of the 1980s – small, powerful, punchy, competitive, South African. Or Stelios Haji-Ioannou, founder of EasyJet, speaking at Reuters – a big man, he stands up and prowls around, describes his empire brilliantly and as a presenter has great lines. When asked 'What advice would you give to any budding entrepreneurs?' he answers 'Have a rich father. Next question.' At this 'brilliant level' you need little help other than to check and recheck that you are keeping up to the mark.

  The world makes superficial judgements – recognise this rather than resent it.

- Brilliant presentations challenge convention. *The World is Flat* is the name of Thomas Friedman's book. It's a great title. It is counter-intuitive in the same way that Edward de Bono's *I am Right and You are Wrong* is, but in the latter instance I have a horrible suspicion that the author actually thought that he *was* right and that we *were* wrong and that he wasn't being ironic at all. Is that true Edward? No. So I am wrong. And you are right.

  Brilliance in presenting is seen frequently in surprising people. Christopher Ricks, professor of humanities at Boston University and Oxford professor of poetry, is a passionate fan of Bob Dylan and argues that *Lay Lady Lay* is from the same poetic blood line as John Donne's love poem called 'Going to Bed' (Elegy XIX). I love the thinking that places Donne in a contemporary context and Dylan in a timeless one. Ricks says it so simply and so brilliantly and he really has the presenter's touch when he says 'Great minds think and feel alike'. If you aspire to brilliance you must be able to make connections like this.

Brilliant presentations change things, and things are changed by an audience being engaged and being persuaded to think and to see things differently. Read the clearest thinkers around, people who try to change minds – Friedman, Ricks, Matthew Parris (on his day), Malcolm Gladwell, Tom Wolfe (still), Anatole Kaletsky, Lucy Kellaway and so on. In a world changing as fast and dramatically as ours, brilliance in presentation is unlikely to come from conventional been-there-seen-that thinking. Yes, the world really is flat.

- Have I Got News for You? This incredibly popular BBC TV series found its inspiration in the news and the apparent improvisational genius of the key players. Some of this, it turns out, is pre-planned – so there goes another Santa Claus legend, deflated and debunked – but some of it is clearly live, for real and very, very funny. We can learn two things from this. Be in touch with the events of the day, anything that might be relevant to your presentation, and understand what the headlines are elsewhere in the world. For instance, just look at www.wnsociety.com and you're living in the global economy. Find the funniest off-the-wall stories – Victor Lewis Smith in *Private Eye*, the *Financial Times* for the occasional blinding insight, and *The Week*. To learn about China visit www.danwei.org; for wonderful American lunacy www.theonion.com; for management stuff try http://fastcompany.com; for innovation and funky ideas www.springwise.com. Brilliance does not come in a room. It comes from walking the street, the shops, talking to people, reading, making connections and, critically, from being prepared to push yourself to think the unthinkable.

If you're going to be brilliant, as I've said before, use the best help you can find – global thinkers, intriguing writers, batty eccentrics – anyone or anything that gets your brain going. Brilliance has opinion so have a few themes that people could get you going on and which could fill a rant of an hour or more. For me, these would currently be China, bullying in the workplace, ensuring that all employees are taught the art of presentation, momentum marketing, the future and how this affects *you*, and why guerrillas will always win. Choose your own themes and have a few 'off the peg' presentations – things you feel strongly about that you can keep up to date with fresh examples and stories.

Brilliance is rarely extempore, it is almost always based on rigorous knowledge, but if you have one of a series of 'passion subjects' to hand and are willing to take the risk then you can run a question and answer session and an 'apparently' improvised show that will amaze people.

- The audience is right or as the president of Orvis once put it: 'The consumer's right even when they are goddamned wrong.' In my experience audiences, on balance, would prefer an agreeable to a boring or dispiriting time. One of the best presentations I did was with Chris Pinnington of Euro RSCG. It was a pitch for a firework safety campaign by the DTI to Baronness Denton. We kept it really short – maybe ten slides, lots of space for questions and answers. She was preoccupied in the tiny room we had to present in at Millbank House opposite the House of Commons and she was constantly looking at the Commons monitor, which shows who's speaking at that moment in each house and on what. People from other agencies complained that she was being ill-mannered and not paying attention but we'd realised that she was speaking in a debate later and was just fitting this in. We won the assignment. We got our audience dead right. We were also very good.

- When it all goes wrong, there are no guarantees. You've researched the venue, prepared the piece, you've got a great story and stunning slides with the best backup team in London who, playing safe, even have two computers. What could possibly go wrong? Wow! Use your imagination:

  - a terrorist attack;

  - a tube strike;

  - a flood;

  - a strike in your own company;

  - a product recall – remember the £20 million Cadbury salmonella problem?;

  - you have laryngitis, flu or a major stomach upset;

  - your deputy chairman dies;

  - a consumer dies from eating your product (and it's in the papers that day);

  - a power cut;

  - a moment of insanity from one of your backup team;

  - the police arrive and arrest your stage manager for non-appearance in court on a driving offence.

Nearly all the disasters I've met have been turned into triumphs by brilliant presenters in flashes of inspiration:

  - they sit down and tell the whole unvarnished story without slides;

  - they turn it all into a question-and-answer session;

  - they get ice-creams in for those who want them;

  - they turn the event into a party – off to the pub and a long conversation;

> ● they take charge in a different way, breaking the audience
>   up into groups and running on-the-spot focus groups.
>
> The real brilliance is in managing situations so you achieve
> solutions that are effective and memorable. I have assumed that
> you are brilliant, and therefore that you will be respected for
> what you can do and achieve. What you will do – being brilliant
> – is to avoid taking anything for granted.

brilliant tip

Brilliant presenters always know when to ask for help

brilliant tip

The real brilliance is in managing situations so you achieve
solutions that are effective and memorable

Summary

The final things that brilliant presenting depends on are:

- Having brilliant people as mentors and advisors. People
  who can help you to turn an ordinary presentation into a
  memorable or even a brilliant one. People whom you trust
  and who understand you. Critically, people who want to
  make you look brilliant.

- Spending enough time to allow you to create brilliant material.

- Using brilliant slide makers.

- Knowing your audience; understanding their mood and
  their needs.

- Liking them; liking them a lot.
- Wanting, really wanting to be brilliant.

Want it with some of the passion (if not with the language) that chef Gordon Ramsay shows. If you sincerely want to be brilliant and are prepared to work at it, brilliant is what you'll become.

CHAPTER 14

So you've made it – brilliant, well done!

B ut can you remember how to do brilliant presentations time after time? I strongly recommend that you read this chapter before every presentation. However brilliant you are. However good everyone said the last presentation was. Take nothing for granted. Read it again and again. It'll stop you making sloppy mistakes or falling back into bad habits. It'll stop you getting cocky. As Jimmy Cliff said 'the bigger they come the harder they fall'. You are at your most vulnerable when you are at your most brilliant. Don't stumble; practise, practise, practise.

This is the brilliant formula

There's nothing magic about this, you just need to listen to the professionals. Follow the 'brilliant presentation' format and work really hard at it. And remember, the idea of a quick fix is appealing but is as misguided in its effect as a crash diet is:

- You need to be honest about how good or bad you are to start with.
- You need to practise really hard to get good.
- You need to devote more time to planning, writing and rehearsing than you could imagine possible.
- The biggest change that you'll notice is that you will begin to *want* to present and, however much you may protest, a certain thrill will fire in your stomach as opposed to a dread

of anticipation. If you've read this book and are prepared to devote time to improvement then it is unlikely that you won't have improved massively already.

This is a very competitive world and there are many very young people who find the act of standing up in front of their peers a lot less alien than it used to be. In modern life, do not underestimate how important and career-defining being a brilliant presenter is. Why? Because people are judged on how they perform in public because it shows:

- how good the company they represent is. The better they are, the better their company seems, the better they seem for representing it;
- how confident they are in their own ability;
- how well prepared they are;
- how knowledgeable they are;
- how attuned they are to their stakeholders;
- how inspirational they are as leaders;
- how responsive and flexible they seem to be;
- how with-it they are.

How with it are you?

In a world shaking up and shaking down as much as ours is, a world in which the 'American dream' declines in the face of the 'Asian explosion', we'd better have a global viewpoint and a sense of why what the *Economist* mischievously called 'Chindia' is so important. These are not just 'emerging economies', they are the future of the world.

Our ability to deal with the new icon of the twenty-first century, St Paradox, and communicate the challenges that exist to those around us in a clear and inspiring way will be what distinguishes the best from the average executive.

Communicating change vividly, with compassion and real understanding will become one of the most vital assets any executive can possess.

Presentation has never been more important

In business, brilliant presentation to stakeholders – workforce, peers, competitors, customers, consumers, suppliers, investors, media, analysts, business experts and opinion formers – has never been so important. Brilliant presentation comes, more than anything else, from clarity of thinking and empathy with the audience, and the clear thinking and understanding that will give us the best chance of building a better world.

The tools of the discipline have been described already – but, as any brilliant presenter will tell you, repetition does not go amiss.

- Decide how good or bad you are. Analyse your strengths and weaknesses. Given how important the art and craft of presentation are, do not try to wriggle away from your shortcomings. Talk to others if you think you are perfect – their comments may be helpful. Get a fix on where you stand and what a reasonable target is. This is about planning your future, not just hoping for the best.

- The context. Spend as long on this as it takes before you ever start thinking about what you are going to say and how you are going to say it. Work out *why* you are doing the presentation, to *whom*, how they *feel* and what they *think*, *what's* going on around them, *where* you are doing it, *how many* will be there. Leave nothing to chance – be very clear about the context in which you are performing. Get your understanding of context wrong and the rest will unravel.

- The story. The message, the big idea. How does it develop? How can you tell it clearly and compellingly? Do you have the 'elevator pitch' or synopsis of the plot absolutely clear –

so were someone to say 'Richard you have only two minutes to do your presentation to us, not half an hour' could you do it? Become a great storyteller and you could become a great leader – it's that simple.

● Splashes of colour. The stuff that enlivens, dramatises and makes it exciting. The bits of contemporary fact, anecdotes, data, evidence that makes the story unforgettable and convincing. These are the spear carriers, the crowds, the extras, the props that make the story more fun. Remember *The Winter's Tale*, 'Exit pursued by a bear' – great stage direction, great fun. But it's more than fun – character, attitude and intelligence add colour and memorability to a show.

● Visual backup. The slides, the staging, the 'toys' you use to make a memorable point. These are there to enhance but never to run the show. Make sure they are good enough so they don't hamper the rest. Learn to do your own by all means but take professional advice when it comes to a big show so that you are up with or ahead of other speakers. Good slides speed you up, make you feel good and keep the audience on your side without demanding too much of them. Be proud of your material; don't accept that it's just good enough, or it almost certainly won't be.

brilliant tip

Do your own slides by all means but when it comes to a big show take professional advice

● The performance. A nerveless tour de force is what you should be aiming for. Tame those butterflies in your stomach, make sure you are in good voice, use coaches to transform you from being apologetic (very bad) into a good-humoured energy source (very good). You are on stage – act like you own the space, the story and, for so long as you are up there, the attention of the audience. Have fun. This is not a board meeting, this is theatre.

- Being in control. You are a control freak or, better still, you are surrounded by control freaks who leave nothing to chance. You have created a brilliantly unusual agenda and you have great takeaways. You are thinking of ways to break the 'me up there and you down here' paradigm. This is your show – go for it. Before, during and after. And if you do this, this audience is yours forever.

Summary

Brilliance will be achieved if . . .

- you decide you really want to enjoy presenting, not just to go through the motions.
- you believe you can.
- you succeed in controlling your nerves.
- you believe life is exciting.
- you have an avid curiosity about everything you read and see.
- you listen as well as you talk.
- you want to be great.
- you realise what other people can do better than you.
- you use their superior skills when it matters.
- you practise.

While I can give you techniques to succeed, I can't give you that desire to excel. But if your desire to be brilliant is obsessive then I think you are going to find that you like presenting a lot pretty soon.

Welcome to the theatre of presentation. Enjoy the buzz.

CHAPTER 15

Applying your skills to smaller meetings

When I first wrote *Brilliant Presentation* I hoped it contained some sound advice and maybe some inspiring tips. Maybe it did, because I've had positive feedback from a lot of people. However, some told me there was an unanswered question. When is a presentation not a presentation? What presentational behaviour is required in a small but crucial meeting? This is my guidance on how to run the meeting of ten or less possibly using paper as a prompt but almost certainly using no slides.

No slides. Why not?

There are times when slides seem wrong. When they suggest that you are not open minded at all; that your mind is made up; that it's locked shut and that you are there just to sell them your point of view. An informal meeting, hopefully of minds, becomes or can become instead, a formal, unproductive or, worse, an antagonistic monologue. I've seen people thinking they were prepared but because of the paraphernalia they bring with them they lose the audience; as Tommy Cooper, late genius-comedian and improviser used to say – 'Just like that'. Small meetings are designed to make things happen, not to be slide shows. The catchphrase 'and here is one I prepared earlier' is to be avoided. Instead you should be aiming for 'and here is one we've created, together, now'.

You've been promoted, so make that first meeting count

Decide what you want them to think about you and about it – your promotion. Without knowing the context of your promotion it's really hard to be helpful. Did your predecessor die of natural causes, commit suicide or were they executed – fired that is, or were they murdered – whistle-blown by colleagues or, alternately, did they go on to higher and grander things. Context is everything. But this is your chance to make an impact so make it.

- Do not be flash.
- Do not show off.
- Do not patronise.

Enough of the do-nots. Do set a clear agenda. Do aim to make decisions. Do try and make the atmosphere relaxed, positive and effective. Do keep it moving along fast. Do try and make them walk out muttering – 'that's more like it'.

You want to be promoted, so lift your game

The biggest reason for executives failing is because they are poor presenters. Work for hours on your own presentation in reducing an argument to five clearly argued minutes. Know your stuff so well you cannot be thrown off your stride. But be kind to yourself – everything falls into threes – three things to comment on – three problems, three opportunities. The 'rule of three' is for you a way of framing arguments and focusing on messages so don't wreck it by continually saying 'three things occur to me' and revealing that you rely on this technique (anyway they might have read this book.) The reason for them promoting you is that you look as though you know what you are doing. The easiest way of making them think this is by being accomplished at talking about what you've done and are doing and why you are doing it.

Be prepared: the key advantage

I was never a boy scout. However, I always thought their slogan was spot on – 'be prepared'. All the people I coach get hammered by me on the issue of preparation. Astonishingly, many people prefer to wing it and this has always seemed to me the utmost in futile hope. You cannot seriously expect the god of presentation to keep on getting you out of the unprepared mess you've created or have just let happen. When all it takes is an hour (or a lot less if you get the hang of it) to get into some sort of shape, not preparing properly is a scandal.

Simply sit down and work out what your audience and colleagues want or expect. Look at all the angles. Read the papers. Think of the questions that need asking and the answers that need giving. Get yourself into a position where the meeting and anything it throws up is not a surprise.

Make your meeting sound as if it's worth going to

Making the meeting sound worth attending is an obvious but effective way of operating. Send out e-mails to tell people how it's going to work. Seek out colleagues ahead of the meeting so unnecessary confrontation is avoided. Make the meeting a highlight in a continuum of discussions. If you have to prepare papers in advance, make sure they get to people in good time and that each topic has a simple one page summary to allow people to get to the nub of things quickly.

Location: choose it, use it, make it memorable

If the meeting isn't in your office or a meeting room, see if you can find somewhere interesting to hold it.

- Outside if it's a beautiful day – why not?
- On the river – if you are near one.

- Somewhere with an inspiring view.
- The War Rooms at Whitehall (if you want to create that sort of drama).
- A room which you've art directed ahead of the event with your products or a wall chart showing all the stakeholders – anything that focuses people on to an issue.
- Somewhere no-one expects to meet but can't get away from. Imagine buying a capsule on the London Eye and holding a half hour meeting there. Awesome above-the-battle stuff.
- A hotel suite – expensive but being there makes a statement that this meeting matters.

Define everyone's expectations. Meet them

Decide exactly why you are holding a meeting, what you want to get out of it, what others want to get out of it, spend ten minutes on working out where the mindset of everyone coming to the meeting is. Imagine what the perfect meeting would be like from everyone's perspective. That's what you should aim for. Always try to meet expectations. It's easy to do. Ask everyone individually what their expectations are ahead of the meeting. Check out that you've met them at the end of the presentation.

Learn to think on your feet

It's easier to do than you'd think yet before you acquire it as a technique it seems an unreachably distant aspiration. There are three parts to it:

1 Having mastery of your brief and the thrust of it not just the (often) distracting detail.
2 Knowing the people and the way they behave. In some companies, challenge is a way of life.

3 Establishing a presence as a performer. It is so much easier to meet than to exceed expectation so establish the way you work and the way you respond. Think about how you want to be seen and heard.

Think about two things – one is being very light on your feet. What is required is nimbleness not dogma. The other is having a clear set of things you believe in; lessons you've learned; principles on which you wouldn't concede. Seeing a performer on stage or in a meeting who is clear about what they stand for is always impressive.

The brilliant executive summary

As people become more senior in business their attention span tends to shorten. As all of us become busier and busier our ability to process information reduces. We all suffer from overload. This is where the executive summary comes into its own.

Those brilliant at it will flourish and get on. And it's easy to do.

- One sentence summarising the issue: simple language, no jargon.
- How radical a change is involved?
- What do we need to consider?
- Who in the organisation does this affect?
- How does it affect them?
- Why is it important, critical, fundamental (whatever it is)?
- When do decisions have to be made and implementation started and completed?
- What are the cost implications (investment, pay back, cost saving, avoidance of risk)?
- Who has to do what and how do they have to do it?
- Summary of the above repeated.

Brand your meetings so they want to come again

How do you brand a meeting? Well you could have a chocolate on each agenda or better a bowl of chopped carrots – for energy. You could have flowers on the table. Pansies would be good. This is what Ophelia said in *Hamlet*: 'These are pansies, they're for thoughts.'

You could have something that symbolises the intent of the meeting. For a cost-cutting meeting you could have a knife (I'm joking). For growth you could have a marrow. For creative brainstorming you could have piles of Smarties or unusual products on the table. For cutting through red tape you could have scissors and red tape or red bureaucracy balloons with pins so you can burst them.

It's very simple. Tangible memory hooks make meetings swing.

Do great minutes

Do them fast and do them brief. Most of all make sure they really reflect the meeting you had, not the meeting you wished you'd had. Stuff like this is all part of the presentation experience.

Have great coffee and backup material

Mark Weinberg appointed FCO as the advertising agency for Allied Hambro, as it was then called, on the strength of its coffee. Things like coffee, fresh orange juice, good biscuits all matter. They reflect how much you care. Presentation is about more than PowerPoint, it's about creating a total experience.

Pre-meetings and post-meetings: how to play the game

When we realise that we are creating a situation that could be called 'presentation for results' we realise it isn't an exercise in presentation craft so much as office politics. The presentation is merely the medium whereby you get the results you want. So make sure you prime people, make sure they are properly briefed and that you follow up with them afterwards.

The game is to move things on. The game is to involve everyone so you get a more intense and productive response. Make sure you make decisions, agree actions and that the participants at this presentation/meeting realise they've been treated seriously.

Enjoy yourself

Make sure they do too.

Meetings should be and can be well crafted events in which the mood is such that you achieve:

- alignment;
- improved thinking;
- a shared mission to communicate more powerfully.

Everything that distinguishes a brilliant presenter on stage can be tuned down to apply to running great meetings that have presentation content. Not only do they work better but they are more fun too.

So enjoy yourself and make sure everyone else enjoys themselves too.

CHAPTER 16

Summary of the lessons in this book

The biggest challenges to brilliance

The biggest challenge starts in the preparation phase. This is when the seeds of disaster can be sown unless you are careful.

First and most important, be very clear why the presentation is being given, who will be in the audience, what their expectations are and how much they know about you.

Second, construct your presentation so it addresses a set of questions and gives clear and understandable answers. Do not talk down to the audience or use jargon. Make sure people know what you are saying and why you are saying it and never let them think in a puzzled way as you finish speaking, 'What was that all about?'

Third, allow twice as much time in preparation as you'd normally expect. Brilliant presenters rarely busk it. They work at their presentation, polishing it, editing it and rehearsing it.

What you must avoid

- Avoid giving yourself too little time to prepare.
- Avoid being self indulgent – remember 'less is more'.
- Avoid being too nervous: you are not going to die up there and you might enjoy it.

- And avoid being cocky. The worst presentations are when the presenter has no nerves at all and comes across as condescending.

My top three brilliant tips

Brilliant tip number 1

Work with professionals – do not try to do your own slides – if it's an event that could influence your career, work with a coach and the top sound and vision operators. Never be guilty of being amateurish. Make sure you rehearse at the venue itself. Do not be taken by surprise.

Brilliant tip number 2

If you want to be remembered, try to find some splashes of colour that make you stand out – a few great facts, a great quote, a topical piece of evidence or a controversial assertion. Be brave.

Brilliant tip number 3

Make a conscious decision to 'like' your audience. Try and give off positive vibes. If you can get on with the audience they'll pay closer attention to you. And yes, you are allowed to smile at them. They are your friends, or they can be your enemies; whichever it is, is up to you.